MW00977076

THE DIVINE POWER OF GOD

RENARDO McCRAY

ISBN: 1490484116
ISBN-13: 978-1490484112

All Scripture quotations are taken from The King James Version of the Bible.

CONTENTS

PREFACE

This book is designed to unlock the mysteries of God. The revelations of God are manifested. The divine power of God is edifying. The divine power of God is anointed. The divine power of God is for such a time as this. The divine power of God is sound doctrine. The divine power of God shines the light on deception. Out the mouth of two or three witnesses every word is established. It draws attention to genuine fellowship. Religion is exposed! The divine power of God, deals with reality. It also paints a picture of exhortation.

Jesus Christ is exalted. God is speaking.

THE DIVINE POWER OF GOD!

DEDICATION

I dedicate this book to the body of Christ.

For as the body is one, and hath many members, and all the members of that one body, being many, are one body: so also is Christ. For by one Spirit are we all baptized into one body, whether we be Jews or Gentiles, whether we be bond or free; and have been all made to drink into one Spirit. For the body is not one member, but many.
1 CORINTHIANS 12:12-14

Patricia Ann Watson, a very special person. She will always be truly missed and loved. She is in the great cloud of witnesses. I thank the Lord, that I will see her again. This book was done in thanksgiving. I'm thankful that Patricia Ann Watson, was a part of my life, and always will be.

ACKNOWLEDGMENTS

I would like to thank my mother, Mae Walden the greatest women I know. Also, my sister, Westine Tunstall for her love; and support. The Labours Of The Harvest: Apostle Clance Jackson, Patricia Kilpatrick, Nathaniel Cherry, Pastor Don Sturiano, Patrick Lavendar Jr.

THE DIVINE POWER OF GOD

JESUS!

CHAPTER 1

UNDERSTANDING THE REALITY OF FAITH

For I am not ashamed of the gospel of Christ: for it is the power of God unto salvation to every one that believeth; to the Jew first, and also to the Greek. (Vs.17) For therein is the righteousness of God revealed from faith to faith: as it is written, The just shall live by faith. – **ROMANS 1:16-17**

Whenever the full gospel is preached the righteousness of God is always revealed. The terminology from faith to faith, is a very vague description, used in our day an age. The term clearly states that faith is obtained when one believes in Jesus Christ as Lord. The faith obtained produces a lifestyle of faithfulness. The just shall live by faith (**HABAKKUK 2:4**). A familiar verse the Apostle Paul used twice in the New Testament, Timothy also used it once as he authored the book of Hebrews.

So then faith cometh by hearing, and hearing by the word of God.
– **ROMANS 10:17**

The highest degree of knowledge we can obtain as it refers to the scriptures, would be to understand that the context is more important than the text.
– **Romans 10:17** in context is referring to the gospel. Many believers, quote this verse with a meaning that the context does not support. Many believers, have wrongly believed, that every time you read the Bible you get more faith. The verse is declaring that faith is obtained through believing the gospel. As believers, we must become students of the scriptures or unbelief will automatically consume us. In other words, you read the Bible to sustain the faith you've obtained. For years I've heard people teach, your prayers don't get answered when you don't have enough faith. A believer's problem never stands in the fact that they don't possess enough faith. A believer's problem would always be structured by unbelief. The faith that is manifested by the gospel is originally saving faith. Many times believers, focus their faith on trying to get things from God. The purpose of being born again is to enter into kingdom living. Being ignorant of what Christ, purchased for all believers, will always keep the children of God small minded.

The natural mind of man, will always result back to trying to earn something from God outside of the Lord Jesus.

THE MEASURE OF FAITH

I beseech you therefore, brethren, by the mercies of God, that ye present your bodies a living sacrifice, holy, acceptable unto God, which is your reasonable service. (Vs.2) And be not conformed to this world: but be ye transformed by the renewing of your mind, that ye may prove what is that good, and acceptable, and perfect, will of God. (Vs.3) For I say, through the grace given unto me, to every man that is among you, not to think of himself more highly than he ought to think; but to think soberly, according as God hath dealt to every man the measure of faith. – **ROMANS 12:1-3**

Notice God, has given to every believer the measure of faith. Many believers, have adopted the concept of there being a greater and lesser faith. The measure of faith that the Father, has dealt to all believers alike is a limited portion!

In other words, you don't need a lot of faith just the measure without any fear, or unbelief, and you'll do great things. The primary objective of obtaining, saving faith is to make a believer faithful to God. The saints of the ancient days were dedicated followers of the Lord Jesus Christ. Did they have something that the modern day body of Christ doesn't? That's absurd! The saints of old understood that nothing was worthy of them renouncing Jesus Christ.

CONTENDING FOR DELIVERED FAITH

Beloved, when I gave all diligence to write unto you of the common salvation, it was needful for me to write unto you, and exhort you that ye should earnestly contend for the faith which was once delivered unto the saints.
– **JUDE 1:3**

Notice, what the Spirit of the Lord said. Contending for the faith that was once delivered to the saints! How did the saints obtain this faith? The glorious church of old obtained the measure of faith through the gospel. The saints of the ancient age understood the full gospel entirely. However, even in the natural realm you can never appropriate what you don't understand.
For instance, no one could bring their car to you, and say fix my radiator; and you could do it without having the experience as an auto mechanic.

It is one thing to hear the gospel. It's a totally different thing to understand it!

O foolish Galatians, who hath bewitched you, that ye should not obey the truth, before whose eyes Jesus Christ hath been evidently set forth, crucified among you? (Vs.2) This only would I learn of you, Received ye the Spirit by the works of the law, or by the hearing of faith?
– **GALATIANS 3:1-2**

What is the hearing of faith? It is the full gospel!

WE OBTAIN THE FAITH OF JESUS CHRIST

Simon Peter, a servant and apostle of Jesus Christ, to them that have obtained like precious faith with us through the righteousness of God and our Saviour Jesus Christ: (Vs.2) Grace and peace be multiplied unto you through the knowledge of God, and of Jesus our Lord, (Vs.3) According as his divine power hath given unto us all things that pertain unto life and godliness, through the knowledge of him that hath called us to glory and virtue: (Vs.4) Whereby are given unto us exceeding great promises: that by these ye might be partakers of the divine nature, having escaped the corruption that is in the world through lust. – **2 PETER 1:1-4**

Faith is obtained through imputed righteousness. The believer receives the righteousness by faith in Jesus Christ. Jesus gives the believer his righteousness as well as his faith. In the mind of God when Jesus died, we died. When Jesus rose from the dead, we rose from the dead. When the Lord Jesus Christ ascended, to sit on the right hand of God, so did all born again believers. A believer's identity has become Christ. The believer is living a resurrected lifestyle in Christ Jesus. We pray in Jesus name because he is our identity. All believers have the same faith, Jesus Christ has, the only difference is his faith is never mixed with unbelief. Selah

CHAPTER 2

NOT OF THIS WORLD

DIVISION

I have given them thy word; and the world hath hated them, because they are not of the world, even as I (Jesus) am not of the world. – **JOHN 17:14**

Born again believers are separated from the world. This means that Satan doesn't have dominion over them. By law, there is a hatred that comes with the separation. Why? The seeds are different. Notice, what the LORD God, said to Satan who was inside of the serpent.

And I will put enmity between thee and the woman, and between thy seed and her seed; it shall bruise thy head, and thou shalt bruise his heel.
– **GENESIS 3:15**

The enmity is between Satan, and the woman. The woman is symbolic of the church. Her seed is symbolic of Christ. The seed of Satan is the seed of disobedience. The dead seed is separated from God. The word enmity means hostility, and hatred. By divine law, there is a natural enmity between light and darkness!

Blessed are ye, when men shall hate you, and when they shall separate you from their company, and shall reproach you, and cast out your name as evil, for the Son of man's sake. (Vs.23) Rejoice ye in that day, and leap for joy: for, behold, your reward is great in heaven: for in the like manner did their fathers unto the prophets. – **LUKE 6:22-23**

Notice, everything takes place for the Son of man's sake. On account of the Son of man, these things take place. The prophets experienced these things. Why? The prophets were connected to God. Notice again, the Lord Jesus Christ didn't say if. He said when. Meaning he promised his disciples these things will happen. This is the law of the seeds. The seed of God allows a believer to be steadfast in love. Love covers a multitude of sins!

Ye are of God, little children, and have overcome them: because greater is he that is in you, than he that is in the world. (Vs.5) They are of the world: therefore speak they of the world, and the world heareth them.
(Vs.6) We are of God: he that knoweth God heareth us; he that is not of God heareth not us. Hereby know we the spirit of truth, and the spirit of error.
– 1 JOHN 4:4-6

Ye are of God, little children, and have overcome them. Them meaning Satan's representatives. First John chapter four opens up making mention of false prophets. It also mentions the spirit of the antichrist. Antichrist means an opponent of the Messiah. Greater is He that is in you than he that is in the world. He that is in you is the kingdom of God. He that is in the world has power over those who have his seed. The kingdom of God is Sovereign!

But if our gospel be hid, it is hid to them that are lost: (Vs.4) In whom the god of this world has blinded the minds of them which believe not, lest the light of the glorious gospel of Christ, who is the image of God, should shine unto them.
– 2 CORINTHIANS 4:3-4

The seed of Satan in an individual will automatically keep him from seeing. The light of the glorious gospel of Christ, is the only way a person can escape the darkness. Satan is the god of this age. Satan has influence over the world systems of this age.
If any man has not the Spirit of Christ, he is none of his (**Romans 8:9**). Those that have the seed of Satan carry out his will throughout the world. It doesn't matter what kind of position a person may hold or how educated they are.

Jesus said unto them, If God were your Father, ye would love me: for I proceeded forth and came from God; neither came I of myself, but he sent me. (Vs.43) Why do ye not understand my speech? Even because ye cannot hear my word. (Vs.44) Ye are of your father the devil, and the lusts of your father ye will do. He was a murderer from the beginning, and abode not in the truth, because there is no truth in him. When he speaketh a lie, he speaketh of his own: for he is a liar, and the father of it. – **JOHN 8:42-44**

Jesus said the lusts of their father they would do.

He didn't say might or probably. The seed they had separated them from the light. He that hates his brother is a murderer. Jesus Christ came from being in one form with God. He put on flesh, and became a man. Jesus made Christ legal on earth. Jesus Christ was not, and is not of this world!

The child was born, but the Son was given. He was born of a virgin. But He was begotten of the Father. He came to manifest his kingdom on the earth. Jesus Christ, came to restore dominion. He was seen slain before the foundation of the world. He was in the world, and though the world was made by him the world knew him not. He was the word that came into being flesh. He came to take the power out of spiritual death!

Paul, an apostle, (not of men, neither by man, but by Jesus Christ, and God the Father, who raised him from the dead;) (Vs.2) And all the brethren which are with me, unto the churches of Galatia: (Vs.3) Grace be to you and peace from God the Father, and from our Lord Jesus Christ, (Vs.4) Who gave himself for our sins, that he might deliver us from this present evil world, according to the will of God and our father: to whom be glory for ever and ever. Amen.
– GALATIANS 1:1-5

Jesus Christ laid down his life as a ransom. Why?
The wages of sin is death (**Romans 6:23**).
A ransom is a price commanded to let the captives go free. Go free, from the dominion of this evil age. Free from the power of Satan. Free from the orderly arrangement of life under his power. In other words, Jesus came to destroy the seed of Satan.

It is called a spirit of disobedience (**Ephesians 2:2**).
It is called a spirit of bondage (**Romans 8:15**).
It is also called a world spirit (**1 Corinthians 2:12**).
This spirit is separated from the light. This spirit is fathered by Satan. This spirit opposes the things of God. This spirit is dominated by darkness. This spirit fulfills the lust of the flesh, and the desires of the mind. This spirit is conformed to this world.

Then Pilate entered into the judgment hall again, and called Jesus, and said unto him, Art thou the King of the Jews? (Vs.34) Jesus answered him, Sayest thou this thing of thyself, or did others tell it thee of me? (Vs.35) Pilate answered, Am I a Jew? Thine own nation and the chief priest have delivered thee unto me: what hast thou done? (Vs.36) Jesus answered, My kingdom is not of this world, then would my servants fight, that I should not be delivered to the Jews: but now is my kingdom not from hence. – **JOHN 18:33-36**

Jesus Christ was in the world, but he operated from another kingdom. Jesus was under God's government authority. In a kingdom the angels fight for the citizens. In a kingdom you're only subject to the power of the government. Citizens of heaven only praise the government. In a kingdom the citizens follow the constitution. The Bible is what we would call our constitution. This is where we get our rights and privileges. The world is under the ruler ship of Satan. Believers are ambassadors for Christ (**1 Corinthians 5:20**). An ambassador is the highest ranking diplomat who represents a nation. This is why believers are called kings and lords. Kings are rulers. Lords are owners. This is why believers are translated from darkness. And they are placed in the kingdom of God's dear son. The Bible is crystal clear about their only being two families of the earth. There are children of God through Christ Jesus. And there are children of Satan through the disobedience of Adam. These seeds are in total opposition one against the other. God sent his only begotten Son, into the world to do two things; restore and separate.

Think not that I am come to send peace, but a sword. (Vs.35) For I am come to set a man at variance against his father, and the daughter in law against her mother in law. (Vs.36) And a man's foes shall be they of his own household. (Vs.37) He that loveth father or mother more than me is not worthy of me: and he that loveth son or daughter more than me is not worthy of me. (Vs.38) And he that taketh not his cross, and followeth after me, is not worthy of me. (Vs.39) He that findeth his life shall lose it: and he that loseth his life for my sake shall find it.
– MATTHEW 10:34-39

In the context, Jesus is addressing Israel. Why would the Lord Jesus Christ say that he came to set their families at variance? Taking up the cross in (Vs.38) meant exposure to death (Self denial).

Those words were symbolic of regeneration. The variance referred to those that would be regenerated, and those that wouldn't be, that alone would bring about the variance. Yes, that's right, even in the families. Jesus, talked about rejecting the persuasions of family members to follow him.

He (Jesus) came to his own (The Jews) and his own received him not. But as many as received him, to them gave he power to become the sons of God, even to them that believe on his name: (Vs.13) Which were born, not of blood, nor of the will of the flesh, nor of the will of man but of God.
– JOHN 1:11-13

Some received Jesus as Christ (The Messiah). But Israel as a whole rejected Christ as the Messiah. This is where the persecution came from. Why? Though Israel was in Covenant with Jehovah, they still possessed the dead seed. The regenerated Christ followers were persecuted, and killed, by none regenerated Jews. This is the law of light, and darkness.

CHAPTER 3

PROSPER

Blessed is the man that walketh not in the counsel of the ungodly, nor standeth in the way of sinners, nor sitteth in the seat of the scornful. (Vs.2) But his delight is in the law of the LORD; and in his law doth he meditate day and night. (Vs.3) And he shall be like a tree planted by the rivers of water, that bringeth forth his fruit in his season; his leaf also shall not wither; and whatsoever he doeth shall prosper.
– **PSALM 1:1-3**

He that covereth his sins shall not prosper: but whoso confesseth and forsaketh them shall have mercy. – **PROVERBS 28:13**

The believer that's in right standing with the LORD is guaranteed to prosper. He that covers his sins cannot prosper. Why? The word is what prospers a believer. The word is what makes a believer advance. Meditating on the word of God allows the natural mind to become subjected.

The mind of Christ automatically causes a believer to do what God does. As well as saying what God says. A believer can never rise above their confession. Every confession will be tested by the enemy. But a believer can't receive from the kingdom without confessing. Sounds like a paradox.

And Joseph was brought down to Egypt; and Potiphar, an officer of Pharaoh, captain of the guard, an Egyptian, bought him of the hands of the Ishmeelites, which had brought him down thither. (Vs.2) And the LORD was with Joseph, and he was a prosperous man; and he was in the house of his master the Egyptian. (Vs.3) And his master saw that the LORD was with him, and that the LORD made all that he did to prosper in his hand. (Vs.4) And Joseph found grace in his sight, and he served him: and he made him overseer over his house, and all that he had he put into his hand.

(Vs.5) And it came to pass from the time that he had made him overseer in his house, and over all that he had, that the LORD blessed the Egyptian's house for Joseph's sake; and the blessing of the LORD was upon all that he had in the house, and in the field. – **GENESIS 39:1-5**

Joseph was a young man that held fast to his confessions. Joseph was given two dreams by the LORD. He confessed his dreams to his brothers. And from that time forward Joseph became acquainted with oppositions. Now who was behind the oppositions? Satan was behind everyone. The confession that survives the test is the one that prospers you. This is a law. This is the law that God, cannot lie. The LORD was with Joseph. Potiphar saw that the LORD was with Joseph, and that everything he did had prospered. Joseph found grace with Potiphar, and he promoted him. This was God's word promoting Joseph. The LORD blessed the house of the Egyptians, because of Joseph.

When Joseph became overseer of everything it switched jurisdictions. Everything Potiphar owned was under the jurisdiction of Pharaoh. When it was given to Joseph's authority it came under God's jurisdiction. God then had a legal right to bless it. The wealth of the sinner is laid up for the just. The Egyptians, never knew that they were just maintaining their wealth for a young Hebrew boy. Joseph became prime minister over all Egypt. Why? He kept the word God placed in his heart. Joseph stayed in alignment with God's authority, and the word promoted him. It's impossible to believe without confessing it.

Get wisdom, get understanding: forget it not; neither decline from the words of my mouth. (Vs.6) Forsake her not, and she shall preserve thee: love her, and she shall keep thee. (Vs.7) Wisdom is the principal thing; therefore get wisdom: and with all thy getting get understanding. (Vs.8) Exalt her, and she shall promote thee: she shall bring thee to honor, when thou dost embrace her.
– **PROVERBS 4:5-8**

Godly wisdom will make a believer skillful. Understanding allows a believer to walk in discernment. The word a believer keeps preserves him. When a believer loves the word, it guards them. Wisdom is the main thing! Notice, what else the word does. The word does the promoting. The word also brings a believer to honor. Many times believers, want to be made prosperous outside of God's word. That's like expecting a whale to start flying. That's absurd! The word you keep will make you prosperous. This is the blessing system. Believers have been made prosperous through the finish works of the Lord Jesus Christ. However, the word makes you a doer. This is the principle of the blessing system.

Only be thou strong and very courageous, that thou mayest observe to do according to all the law, which Moses my servant commanded thee: turn not from it to the right hand or to the left, that thou mayest prosper whithersoever thou goest. (Vs.8) This book of the law shall not depart out of thy mouth; but thou shalt meditate therein day and night, that thou mayest observe to do according to all that is written therein: for then thou shalt make thy way prosperous, and then thou shalt have good success.
– **JOSHUA 1:7-8**

Even though this was under the Old Covenant the principle is still the same. Jesus came not to destroy the law or the prophets. He came to fulfill them. Meaning everything the prophets prophesied about him. The Lord Jesus Christ fulfilled the law by keeping it without ever breaking it. However, by meditating on the word, it causes a believer to do what he meditates on. God said meditate day and night! For then thou shalt make thy way prosperous, and have good success. The word is what does it all! These words were given to Joshua at the beginning of his ministry. God has told many believers to start their own companies. Or get into real estate, and they fail to do it. This is why many believers never prosper. Prosperity is more than money!

Thou wilt keep him in perfect peace, whose mind is stayed on thee: because he trusteth in thee. – **ISAIAH 26:3**

Peace means to be at peace with God. This signifies oneness. There's no prosperity when a person is not in good health. There's no prosperity when a person is dominated by stress. There's no prosperity when a person is not advancing in life. There's no prosperity outside of fellowship with God period. The word prosperity means wholly.

Let them shout for joy, and be glad, that favor my righteous cause: yea, let them say continually, Let the LORD be magnified, which hath pleasure in the prosperity of his servant.
– **PSALM 35:27**

Prosperity is God's will for his Saints. Dominion means to rule. Rule over stress. Rule over bad health. Rule over poverty. God's will is that his children are wholly!

Beloved, I wish above all things that thou mayest prosper and be in health, even as thy soul prospereth. – **3 JOHN 1:2**

The key to a prosperous life must be wrought through the mind. This mind is in full agreement with the will of the LORD. Prosperity is something that comes from a renewed mind. A renewed mind conforms to the ways of the kingdom of God. The mind has to continually be renewed. Why? The mind is not saved.

Wherefore lay apart all filthiness and superfluity of naughtiness, and receive with meekness the engrafted word, which is able to save your souls. **–JAMES 1:21**

He restoreth my soul: He leadeth me in paths of righteousness for his name's sake.
– PSALM 23:3

Notice, James said through the Holy Spirit, the engrafted word received is able to save the soul. The word save there means to keep safe, heal, deliver, and protect. Then notice what King David said through the Holy Spirit. He restores my soul and leads me in the paths of righteousness for his name's sake. The word restoreth there means to return to the starting point. So we can read it like this. He (God) through his word restores my soul back to the place of Adam's before he sinned. And by the soul being restored, he is able to walk in paths of righteousness. Just as Adam did before he committed high treason. So then we see prosperity through the word of God, is actually living from the kingdom of heaven; manifesting God's will in the earth. There is no sickness in heaven. There is no stress neither is their poverty. There sure isn't any sin. All born again Christians, have been translated into the kingdom of God's dear son. We are called to operate from the right hand of God through Christ Jesus our LORD.

If ye then be risen with Christ, seek those things which are above, where Christ sitteth on the right hand of God. – **COLOSSIANS 3:1**

Whenever the soul is subjected by the word of God, the believer can seek those things that are in alignment, with the resurrected life of Christ Jesus.

CHAPTER 4

WORSHIP THE LORD

I will worship toward thy holy temple, and praise thy name for thy loving kindness and for thy truth: for thou hast magnified thy word above all thy name. – **PSALM 138:2**

Worship is exalting God for who he is. Praise is thanking God for what he has done. However, worship and praise are not based on being in a service. It is scriptural for that to happen. So that is something that most take place. However, praise and worship is something that's done with the heart. Notice, the Psalmist says I will praise, and worship. This deals with a heart that has bowed to the LORD.

Worship is not something we enter into. Worship is a lifestyle. Worship is a fixation! Worship means to pay homage to. It means to reverence. Lying prostrate is an outward expression that bears witness of an inward essence. Worship is not about finding a temple. We are the temple of God.

WORSHIP IS DUE UNTO THE LORD

Give unto the LORD the glory due unto his name; worship the LORD in the beauty of holiness.
– **PSALM 29:2**

Give unto the LORD the glory due unto his name: bring an offering, and come before him: worship the LORD in the beauty of holiness.
– **1 CHRONICLES 16:29**

Worshipping the LORD in the covering of holiness is due unto his name. Imputed righteousness allows us to magnify the LORD by resemblance. The beauty of holiness is like a cloak that keeps a believer covered from the impurities of the world. This cloak protects the heart. The LORD has created a system where he can perpetually see his reflection. We bring the LORD offerings just so our hearts do not cling to anything more than him.

This is the LORD'S definition of worship. He must be above all else. Notice what Abraham said when he was told to offer up Isaac.

And Abraham said unto his young men, Abide ye here with the ass; and I and the lad will go yonder and worship, and come again to you.
– **GENESIS 22:5**

TRUE WORSHIPPERS

Jesus saith unto her, Woman, believe me, the hour cometh, when ye shall neither in this mountain, nor yet at Jerusalem, worship the Father. (Vs.22) Ye worship ye know not what: we know what we worship: for salvation is of the Jews. (Vs.23) But the hour cometh, and now is, when the true worshippers shall worship the Father in spirit and in truth: for the Father seeketh such to worship him. (Vs.24) God is a Spirit: and they that worship him must worship him in spirit and in truth.
– **JOHN 4:21-24**

Jesus Christ here closes the door on a whole dispensation. The Samaritans, worshipped what they knew not. That statement is twofold. One the Samaritans, worshipped idols (**2 Kings 17:29**). Two the Samaritans, tried serving God and idols as well
(**2 Kings 17:41**). God is a Spirit. God seeks those that would worship him in spirit, and in truth. For an unbeliever this would mean conversion. For a believer this would mean being under the blood. Many times believers think they can enter God's presence by worship songs. No song will get a believer in God's presence. No location will put a believer in God's presence.

If we confess our sins, he is faithful and just to forgive us our sins, and to cleanse us from all unrighteousness. – **1 JOHN 1:9**

This is a truth to staying in the LORD'S presence. A believer has to be cleansed to be in the LORD'S presence. This is what the Lord meant by true worshippers. God is a Spirit, and a believer's spirit must be joined to him. This is the power of the blood of the Lord Jesus Christ. His blood cleanses! Many times the service is packed, but many believers are not in his presence. Sin has to be confessed. A believer in sin can sing a hundred songs, and he still will not enter the LORD'S presence.

This doctrine is taught. What do you hear in the Sunday meetings? Come on everyone lets worship, and get into God's presence. It's very possible for someone to sing hymns with un-forgiveness inside of their heart. This is why God said, He looks on the heart.

This people draweth nigh unto me with their mouth, and honoureth me with their lips; but their heart is far from me. (Vs.9) But in vain they do worship me, teaching for doctrines the commandments of men.
– **MATTHEW 15:8-9**

THE LAW OF WORSHIP

And the devil said unto him, All this power will I give thee, and the glory of them: for that is delivered unto me; and to whomsoever I will I give it. (Vs.7) If thou therefore wilt worship me, all shall be thine. (Vs.8) And Jesus answered and said unto him, Get thee behind me, Satan: for it is written, Thou shalt worship the Lord thy God, and him only shalt thou serve. – **LUKE 4:6-8**

Satan has always wanted to be worshipped. This doesn't mean someone singing him a song. Satan tried to tempt Jesus with everything Adam had delivered to him. Notice, Jesus said it is written. (Vs.8) Thou shalt worship the Lord thy God, and him only shalt thou serve. Worship and serve cannot be done apart. However, it is written means worship is a law.

Every human being has to worship something or somebody. So when people are not worshipping God, they have to worship something. Every nation in the Bible, worshipped idols. One of the works of the flesh is idolatry. A law governs behaviors and actions. Not worshipping God allows another substitution to take place. A person will worship a car. A person will worship a house. A person will worship a celebrity. A person will worship money. Adam worshipped Eve!

FELLOWSHIP

If there be therefore any consolation in Christ, if any comfort of love, if any fellowship of the Spirit, if any bowels and mercies, (Vs.2) Fulfil ye my joy, that ye be like minded, having the same love, being of one accord, of one mind.
– **PHILIPPIANS 2:1-2**

If we say that we have fellowship with him, and walk in darkness, we lie, and do not the truth: (Vs.7) But if we walk in the light, as he is in the light, we have fellowship one with another, and the blood of Jesus Christ his Son cleanseth us from all sin.
– 1 JOHN 1:6-7

Fellowship with the Lord allows us to walk in the light. When we are in fellowship with him we are conformed to his image. When we are not in fellowship with him we operate in the nature of the flesh. Walking in the flesh will bring about pride, and selfishness. Walking in the Spirit will bring about humility, and love. It's impossible to manifest the glory of the Lord outside of his presence. Fellowship with the Lord will allow us to give people God encounters. The fruit of the Spirit is the life, and nature of God being manifested through a believer. That is worshipping the Lord! We don't enter his presence. We worship from his presence!

SINGING UNTO THE LORD

Wherefore be ye not unwise, but understanding what the will of the Lord is. (Vs.18) And be not drunk with wine, wherein is excess; but be filled with the Spirit; (Vs.19) Speaking to yourselves in psalms and hymns and spiritual songs, singing and making melody in your heart to the Lord; (Vs.20) Giving thanks always for all things unto God and the Father in the name of our Lord Jesus Christ; (Vs.21) Submitting yourselves one to another in the fear of God.
– EPHESIANS 5:17-21

Notice, one of the applications of being imbued with the Spirit is singing, and making melody in the heart (human spirit) to the Lord. In other words, through fellowship the Holy Spirit permeates the human spirit, and divine worship is celebrated. Now let's notice, that singing the spiritual songs are always generated by the Holy Spirit's fellowship.

Paul and Silas thrust into the inner prison with their feet firmly fastened. And at midnight Paul and Silas prayed, and sang praises unto God: and the prisoners heard them. **– ACTS 16:25**

CHAPTER 5

ENEMIES NEED PRAYER

Woe unto you, when all men shall speak well of you! For so did their fathers to the false prophets. (Vs.27) But I say unto you which hear, Love your enemies, do good to them which hate you, (Vs.28) Bless them that curse you, and pray for them which despitefully use you. – **LUKE 6:26-28**

Ye have heard that it hath been said, Thou shalt love thy neighbor, and hate thin enemy. (Vs.44) But I say unto you, Love your enemies, bless them that curse you, do good to them that hate you, and pray for them which despitefully use you, and persecute you; (Vs.45) That ye may be the children of your Father which is in heaven: for he maketh his sun to rise on the evil and on the good, and sendeth rain on the just and on the unjust. (Vs.46) For if ye love them which love you, what reward have ye? Do not even the publicans the same? (Vs.47) And if ye salute your brethren only, what do ye more than others? Do not even the publicans so? (Vs.48) Be ye therefore perfect, even as your Father which is in heaven is perfect.
– **MATTHEW 5:43-48**

Being able to pray for your enemies is self-evident that you're a child of God. Praying for your enemies also shows that you're perfect. The word perfect means to be mature, in godliness without partiality. Greeting everyone is also a sign of completeness in God. God is whole! Partiality is a sign of religion, not kingdom living. Kingdom living is abnormal!

LOVE THY ENEMIES

Loving our enemies is God's will. Loving the enemies take place when a believer is controlled by the Holy Spirit. God is love! When you, love your enemies, your prayers for them will be fervent. God wants us to intercede for our enemies. Why? Number one, it stops judgment. Number two, it's God's will. Number three, it conforms us to be like God.

Then they cried out with a loud voice, and stopped their ears, and ran upon him with one accord, (Vs.58) And cast him out of the city, and stoned him: and the witnesses laid down their clothes at a young man's feet, whose name was Saul. (Vs.59) And they stoned Stephen, calling upon God, and saying, Lord Jesus, receive my spirit. (Vs.60) And he kneeled down, and cried with a loud voice, Lord, lay not this sin to their charge. And when he had said this, he fell asleep. – **ACTS 7:57-60**

And there followed him a great company of people, and of women, which also bewailed and lamented him. (Vs.28) But Jesus turning unto them said, Daughters of Jerusalem, weep not for me, but weep for yourselves, and for your children. (Vs.29) For, behold, the days are coming, in the which they shall say, Blessed are the barren, and the wombs that never bare, and the paps which never gave suck. (Vs.30) Then shall they begin to say to the mountains, Fall on us; and to the hills, Cover us. (Vs.31) For if they do these things in a green tree, what shall be done in the dry? (Vs.32) And there were also two other, malefactors, led with him to be put to death. (Vs.33) And when they were come to the place, which is called Calvary, there they crucified him, and the malefactors, one on the right hand, and the other on the left. (Vs.34) Then said Jesus, Father, forgive them; for they know not what they do. And they parted his raiment, and cast lots. – **LUKE 23:27-34**

The leading of the Spirit will always fulfill God's will. Empowered by God's Spirit, will always manifest his nature. God's will is that we respond to circumstances, the way he responded to us. The LORD is the God of peace. Peace means to set at one again!
The word peace is twofold. First, it refers to the peace the gospel fashions. Second, it means being quick to forgive.

Blessed are the peacemakers: for they shall be called the children of God.
– **MATTHEW 5:9**

God wants us to do good to our enemies. Why? It protects a believer's heart. Blessing our enemies will disarm Satan.

If thine enemy be hungry, give him bread to eat; and if he is thirsty, give him water to drink: (Vs.22) For thou shalt heap coals of fire upon his head, and the LORD shall reward thee.
– **PROVERBS 25:21-22**

God rewards us for giving to our enemies. Why? It makes us genuinely like him. This giving is done in secret.

When you truly give you don't tell everyone what you did! Be not, as the hypocrites (**Matt. 6:1-4**). To heap coals of fire upon his head is an idiom. It means to awaken your enemy's dead conscience. Why? He has no idea of what he's doing. A dead conscience doesn't care. God desires that all men be saved.

When a man's ways pleases the LORD, he maketh even his enemies to be at peace with him.
– PROVERBS 16:7

When a believer's ways are in agreement with God's word, it brings about oneness. Notice the LORD brings about this oneness. That implies that the LORD becomes involved with the conscience of the enemy. God is about bringing peace. He is the God of peace. Many of times Christians, tend to live in such a way, as if Jesus only died for the church.

For when we were yet without strength, in due time Christ died for the ungodly. (Vs.7) For scarcely for a righteous man will one die: yet peradventure for a good man some would even dare to die. (Vs.8) But God commendeth his love toward us, in that, while we were yet sinners, Christ died for us.
– ROMANS 5:6-8

For God so loved the world, that he gave his only begotten Son, that whosoever believeth in him should not perish, but have everlasting life.
– JOHN 3:16

Christ died for the ungodly. Christ died for the whole world. We are just the ones that received the sacrificial offering. After Adam committed high treason there was no one on earth righteous. It was so bad that God had to become a man. This is why God, even uses his believers to bless their enemies. It is God's will that we pray for them. Why? This is a ministry of reconciliation in a whole different form. Bless those that curse you. Bless means to invoke good upon. It is a benediction. What's the best thing that can be invoked upon a sinner? The Spirit of God draws them to salvation. After all, no one can come unless he is drawn. Selah

CHAPTER 6

THE HOLY SPIRIT IS THE KINGDOM

Then shall the King say unto them on his right hand, Come, ye blessed of my Father, inherit the kingdom prepared for you from the foundation of the world (Vs.35) For I was hungry, and ye gave me meat: I was thirsty, and ye gave me drink: I was a stranger, and ye took me in: (Vs.36) Naked, and ye clothed me: I was sick, and ye visited me: I was in prison, and ye came unto me.
– **MATTHEW 25:34-36**

The kingdom was prepared before the foundation of the world. The kingdom of God, is a very vague term. Many believers, don't understand the kingdom. Before there was an earth the kingdom was established. The New Jerusalem is inside of God right now (**Rev. 21:2**). The kingdom of God is where ever he dwells. The kingdom of God, is a foundation of power. The kingdom is the government of heaven reigning on earth. The kingdom, is a king impacting a domain with his will and intentions. The Spirit of Christ is the kingdom!

THE REASON MAN WAS MADE

And God said, Let us make man in our image, after our likeness: and let them have dominion over the fish of the sea, and over the fowl of the air, and over the cattle, and over all the earth, and over every creeping thing that creepeth upon the earth.
– **GENESIS 1:26**

God made a physical earth, so a man could rule it. Man was made only to reign on earth! The Father, the Word, and the Holy Spirit, all agreed. God manifested on earth, what he had already done in his Spirit. Let them have dominion! The word dominion means, subjugate. Subjugate means to bring under the domination or control. In other words, God said Adam control the world. Adam was a king!

THE FORFEITED KINGDOM

For God doth know that in the day ye eat thereof, then your eyes shall be opened, and ye shall be as gods, knowing good and evil. (Vs.6) And when the woman saw that the tree was good for food, and that it was pleasant to the eyes, and a tree to be desired to make one wise, she took of the fruit thereof, and did eat, and gave also unto her husband with her; and he did eat.
– **GENESIS 3:5-6**

Adam was given a commandment, to protect his influence. The commandment God gave Adam was supposed to leave Satan ineffective. Adam was given delegated authority over Satan. Adam transgressed God's commandment. This means Adam deliberately rebelled. Adam had forfeited his influence before he ate. Notice (Vs.6) she took of the fruit thereof, and did eat; and gave also to her husband with her, and he did eat. Adam didn't come from work, and get tricked. Adam listened to Eve, being deceived. Adam violated God's dominion principle!

THE PROMISE TO RESTORE KINGDOM

And I (God) will put enmity between thee and the woman, and between thy seed and her seed; it shall bruise thy head, and thou shalt bruise his heel.
– **GENESIS 3:15**

The woman is symbolic of the church. Her seed is symbolic of Christ (**Galatians 3:16**). Enmity is between the church, and Satan. The Christian has enmity against the dead seed. Satan has enmity against the living seed. This is why light, and darkness naturally separates. The woman's seed will crush Satan's dominion. Adam gave Satan dominion (**Luke 4:6**). Satan will bruise his heel. That term describes the torcher that the body of Jesus would endure on the cross.

For unto us a child is born, unto us a son is given: and the government shall be upon his shoulder and his name shall be called Wonderful, Counsellor, The mighty God, The everlasting Father, The Prince of Peace. (Vs.7) Of the increase of his government and peace there shall be no end, upon the throne

of David, and upon his kingdom, to order it, and to establish it with judgment and with justice from henceforth even for ever. The zeal of the LORD of hosts will perform this.
– ISAIAH 9:6-7

Isaiah prophesied, about everything that was already done in the Spirit. Jesus came to earth, with the government on his shoulders. The government is the Holy Spirit. The increase of God's empire, and oneness shall be no end. God's initial plan was to make earth a colony. What is a colony? A colony is a district territory ruled by a kingdom.

The kingdom is in the Spirit. God has always desired for his people to reign on earth. Adam was supposed to rule Eden, from his inside out. Everything Adam ever needed was inside of him.

THE KINGDOM OF GOD IS WITHIN

For the kingdom of God is not meat and drink; but righteousness, and peace in the Holy Spirit
– ROMANS 14:17

And when he was demanded of the Pharisees, when the kingdom of God should come, he answered them and said, The kingdom of God cometh not with observation: (Vs.21) Neither shall they say, Lo here! Or, lo there! For, behold, the kingdom of God is within you.
– LUKE 17:21

Jesus said the kingdom of God, cometh not with observation. The kingdom of God, is close to the natural eyes. The kingdom of God, deals with vision. The kingdom of God, is a type of life. Righteousness means innocent. Peace means set at one again. Joy means cheerful. The word kingdom means sovereign. Sovereign means a supreme ruler. The life in the Holy Spirit is superior. The Holy Spirit can rule over bondage. The Holy Spirit can rule over poverty. The Holy Spirit can rule over Satan. The Holy Spirit is the government. The kingdom of God is now!

THE GOSPEL JESUS PREACHED

Now after that John was put in prison, Jesus came into Galilee, preaching the gospel of the kingdom of God, (Vs.15) And saying, The time is fulfilled, and the kingdom of God is at hand: repent ye, and believe the gospel.
– **MARK 1:14-15**

And Jesus went about all the cities and villages, teaching in their synagogues, and preaching the gospel of the kingdom, and healing every sickness and every disease among the people.
– **MATTHEW 9:35**

The priority of Jesus was the kingdom. Jesus never preached any other gospel! Notice, he preached first. Second, he healed all manner of sickness, and disease, among the people. The healings were evidence of the gospel he preached. God confirmed the gospel, Jesus preached. Where did the gospel come from? The gospel came from God. The gospel deals with dominion power. Jesus didn't come to deal with death. Jesus came to take the power out of death. Many Christians, preach what Jesus did, not the gospel he preached. Jesus preached the full counsel of God.

And he (Jesus) said unto them, I must preach the kingdom of God to other cities also: for therefore am I sent. **LUKE 4:43**

The former treatise have I made, O Theophilus, of all that Jesus began both to do and teach, (Vs.2) Until the day in which he was taken up, after that he through the Holy Spirit had given commandments unto the apostles whom he had chosen: (Vs.3) To whom also he shewed himself alive after his passion by many infallible proofs, being seen of them forty days, and speaking of the things pertaining to the kingdom of God: (Vs.4) And, being assembled together with them, commanded them that they should not depart from Jerusalem, but wait for the promise of the Father, which, saith he, ye have heard of me. – **ACTS 1:1-4**

Jesus declared the reason he was sent was to preach the kingdom of God. Jesus spoke with his apostles' forty days after his resurrection, about the kingdom of God. Jesus started his earthly ministry with the kingdom gospel.

Jesus ended his earthly ministry, with the kingdom gospel. The gospel is the government of heaven!

POWER IS THE PROOF

For the kingdom of God is not in word, but in power.
– **1 CORINTHIANS 4:20**

These twelve Jesus sent forth, and commanded them, saying, Go not into the way of the Gentiles, and into any city of the Samaritans enter ye not: (Vs.6) But go rather to the lost sheep of the house of Israel. (Vs.7) And as ye, Go preach, saying, The kingdom of heaven is at hand (Vs.8) Heal the sick, cleanse the lepers, raise the dead, cast out devils: freely ye have received, freely give.
– **MATTHEW 10:5-8**

If I do not the works of my Father, believe me not. (Vs.38) But if I do, though ye believe not me, believe the works: that ye may know, and believe, that the Father is in me, and I in him.
– **JOHN 10:37-38**

Jesus said the works that the Father, did through him was the evidence that he, and the Father; were in union. God's Spirit working through a believer will always take dominion over an environment and change the atmosphere. Notice, the mandate Jesus gives to his disciples in (**MATTHEW 10:8**). Heal the sick, cleanse the lepers, raise the dead, cast out devils: freely ye have received, freely give. Jesus didn't tell them to go, and pray about it first. Jesus said go, and do. What did they receive freely? The ability to operate under the dominion power that Jesus was under. Jesus only did, and said what he seen the Father, doing and saying. The disciples going, and proclaiming that the kingdom of heaven, was at hand was releasing the words of life. The words they released were the words the Father, had said.

It is the Spirit that quickeneth, the flesh profiteth nothing, the words that I speak unto you; they are Spirit, and they are life (**JOHN 6:63**). Whenever the Lord Jesus spoke, he released the life of God's Spirit into the environment. And the results equaled God's dominion on earth. The supremacy of heaven is based on God himself. All the love, joy, and everything that the realm of heaven inhabits is a reality because of God's presence.

Notice, what the Apostle Paul said through the Holy Spirit to the church in Corinth.

And I, brethren, when I came to you, came not with excellency of speech or of wisdom, declaring unto the testimony of God. (Vs.2) For I determined not to know any thing among you, save Jesus Christ, and him crucified. (Vs.3) And I was with you in weakness, and in fear, and in much trembling. (Vs.4) And my speech and my preaching was not with enticing words of man's wisdom, but in demonstration of the Spirit and of power: (Vs.5) That your faith should not stand in the wisdom of men, but in the power of God.
– 1 CORINTHIANS 2:1-5

The Apostle Paul preached, and taught the gospel through his whole ministry. The gospel is the power of God. The Holy Spirit works exclusively, in agreement with the finished work of the cross. Notice (Vs.4) demonstration of the Spirit and of power. In other words, the gospel revealed the power of the Spirit. The whole Bible, is about one message the gospel. Now Paul, through Jesus Christ, was given revelation on how to teach it from many different aspects.

For I am not ashamed of the gospel of Christ: for it is the power of God unto salvation to every one that believeth; to the Jew first, and also to the Greek. (Vs.17) For therein is the righteousness of God revealed from faith to faith: as it is written, The just shall live by faith. **–ROMANS 1:16-17**

Every time the gospel is preached the power of God's Spirit is released. The gospel reveals the righteousness of God, and in it faith is released when one receives the gift. The just shall live by faith (**HABAKKUK 2:4**). The just shall live by the faith they obtained through the gospel. Where does the church go wrong? We don't teach the gospel in the church. It is the only thing the Apostle Paul did. Preaching means to proclaim, and teaching means to explain.

CHAPTER 7

THE TRUTH ABOUT SATAN

Satan is not like a human being that's trying to serve God, and make it into heaven. He was in heaven as Lucifer. When Lucifer was cast out of heaven, then he became Satan. How could he go from being in God's presence, and then become consumed by evil? Any spirit that is disconnected from God naturally dies spiritually. God is the Spirit of life. Jesus said that the devil was a murderer from the beginning, and abode not in the truth, because there was no truth in him (**John 8:44**). The thing that consumed Lucifer was pride. Pride is a controlling action. This action derives from the desire to be self-exalted. Pride will separate anyone from God. Why? God can't be God, for a proud spirit. Humility is a spirit that is submitted to God. A proud spirit cannot be submissive because it determines to be first. This is why the word says God, resist the proud, but gives grace to the humble (**James 4:6**). However, Satan is a complete evil angelic being. Jesus has defeated Satan by his death, burial, and resurrection. So that the children of God, may freely have restored to them what was loss. What did the man lose? Man lost dominion over the earth through God's Spirit.

THE WORD CREATED EVERYTHING

Praise ye the LORD. Praise ye the LORD from the heavens: praise him in the heights. (Vs.2) Praise ye him, all his angles: praise ye him, all his host. (Vs.3) Praise ye him, sun and moon: praise him, all ye stars of light. (Vs.4) Praise him, ye heavens of heavens, and ye waters that be above the heavens. (Vs.5) Let them praise the name of the LORD: for he commanded, and they were created.
– PSALM 148:5

Giving thanks unto the Father, which hath made us meet to be partakers of the inheritance of the saints in light: (Vs.13) Who hath delivered us from the power of darkness, and hath translated us into the kingdom of his dear Son: (Vs.14) In whom we have redemption through his blood, even the forgiveness of sins: (Vs.15) Who is the image of the invisible God, the firstborn of every

creature: (Vs.16) For by him were all things created, that are in heaven, and that are in earth, visible and invisible, whether they be thrones, or power: all things were created by him, and for him: (Vs.17) And he is before all things, and by him all things consist.
- COLOSSIANS 1:12-17

God never created anything without the Word. All the angelic beings were created by the Word. This involves the angels that were cast out of heaven. These are the ones we know today as evil spirits or evil beings. Lucifer who came into being Satan was an archangel. Or a cherub you might have called him. However, Satan never wanted to submit to God's authority from the beginning. Being that he was created by the Word, he is programmed to follow it. It's like a robot that's created to be controlled by certain words. This is why Satan comes to steal the Word from a believer. Why? Satan knows if he steals the Word he steals a believer's authority. When a believer speaks the Word in faith, it's just as if God said it.

Thou believest that there is one God; thou doest well: the devils also believe, and tremble.
– JAMES 2:19

And in the synagogue there was a man, which had a spirit of an unclean devil, and cried out with a loud voice, (Vs.34) Saying, Let us alone; what have we to do with thee, thou Jesus of Nazareth? Art thou come to destroy us? I know thee who thou art; the Holy One of God.
– LUKE 4:33-34

Satan and his hierarchy understand that there's one God. They also understand that the Word is God. Notice, they anticipate judgment through fear. Satan and his hierarchy believe that God cannot lie. They believe his authority is supreme. They witnessed this through experience instead of submitting. They are prime examples! One thing a believer has to understand is that these evil forces believe God. The only thing is that their believing doesn't come with obedience from reverence. They work to oppose the Word of God so they will not have to submit.

And I will put enmity between thee and the woman, and between thy seed and her seed; it shall bruise thy head, and thou shalt bruise his heel.
– GENESIS 3:15

Now, after the LORD God, made this declaration it was the only thing Satan thought about. Satan knows what God says will come to pass. Although Satan's all-out attempts were to try to oppose it. This is the same thing Satan does in a believer's life. He tries to stop the Word of God from manifesting. As believers, we are only supposed to say what God said! The victory is already ours. The battle is already won. However, our job is to persistently tread upon conquered foes!

And the king took his ring from his hand, and gave it unto Haman the son of Hammedatha the Agagite, the Jews' enemy. (Vs.11) And the king said unto Haman, The silver is given to thee, the people also, to do with them as it seemeth good to thee. (Vs.12) Then were the king's scribes called on the thirteenth day of the first month, and there was written according to all that Haman had commanded unto the king's lieutenants, and to the governors that were over every province, and to the rulers of every people of every province according to the writing thereof, and to every people after their language; in the name of king Ahasuerus was it written, and sealed with the king's ring. (Vs.13) And the letters were sent by posts into all the king's provinces, to destroy, to kill, and to cause to perish, all Jews, both young and old, little children and women, in one day, even upon the thirteenth day of the twelfth month, which is the month Adar, and to take the spoil of them for a prey. (Vs.14) The copy of the writing for a commandment to be given in every province was published unto all people, that they should be ready against that day. (Vs.15) The posts went out, being hastened by the king's commandment, and the decree was given in Shushan the palace. And the king and Haman sat down to drink; but the city Shushan was perplexed.
– ESTHER 3:10-15

Satan attempts to destroy the entire Jewish lineage. Satan wanted to stop the lineage of the Jewish people. Why? The enemy understands that when the LORD God says something his integrity is involved. Haman the noble official of the Persian Empire, was just an instrument that Satan deliberately used. The Jewish people had the LORD's name on them. God is the Alpha, and the Omega, the beginning; and the end. Although the Israelites were rewarded with captivity for rebellion as they were in the days of the king Ahasuerus.

And he (The LORD) said unto Abram, Know of a surety that thy seed shall be a stranger in a land that is not theirs, and shall serve them; and they shall afflict them four hundred years; (Vs.14) And also that nation, whom they shall serve, will I judge: and afterward shall they come out with great substance.
– GENESIS 15:13-14

The LORD, made a covenant with Abram before Israel, even came into being a nation. The Messiah, had to have a lineage to come through. Esther was made queen before Haman's evil scheme against the Jews. Esther saved the entire Jewish nation. The LORD'S integrity was involved. Faith is the ability to see what's already done. Believers are supposed to control Satan.

THE ATTEMPT TO KILL THE CHILD

Then Herod, when he saw that he was mocked of the wise men, was exceeding wroth, and sent forth, and slew all the children that were in Bethlehem, and in all the coasts thereof, from two years old and under, according to the time which he had diligently inquired of the wise men. (Vs.17) Then was fulfilled that which was spoken by Jeremy the prophet, saying, (Vs.18) In Rama was there a voice heard, lamentation, and weeping, and great mourning, Rachel weeping for her children, and would not be comforted, because they are not. (Vs.19) But when Herod was dead, behold, an angle of the Lord appeared in a dream to Joseph in Egypt, (Vs.20) Saying, Arise, and take the young child and his mother, and go into the land of Israel: for they are dead which sought the young child's life.
– MATTHEW 2:16-20

Satan diligently tried to stop the Messiah from manifesting. Herod and Haman both died in an attempt to nullify the Lord's promise. God prophesied this event through Jeremiah his prophet.

Thus saith the LORD; a voice was heard in Ramah, lamentation, and bitter weeping; Rachel weeping for her children refused to be comforted for her children, because they were not.
– JEREMIAH 31:15

Believers are supposed to stand on the Word. God lives in eternity which means he's not subject to time. So whenever the LORD speaks, it's already done. The Word of God is something that is already done. So when we believe it, we are able to bring eternity into time.

Notice, the LORD spoke about Rachel weeping for her children in the days of Jeremiah. He is the Alpha, and the Omega. He is the beginning, and the end. He is the first, and the last. The prophets spoke under divine inspiration. They foretold events. The Bible is a book about prophecy. There is something that God can't help, he knows everything. Nothing ever occurs to God. He never looks at his right hand to Christ Jesus, and says you seen that. This is why all believers are supposed to say what the LORD says. Everything He said is already done. This is why God can give you a vision and it comes to pass. A vision is nothing more than God, brings the future to your present time. Many times believers go wrong trying to get God to do what he has already done. For instance, many of God's people are sick, and they try to get him to heal them. Instead of receiving their healing that God wrought through Christ two thousand years ago. The Bible declares that by his (Jesus) stripes **WE ARE HEALED (ISAIAH 53:5**). It doesn't say anything about he's going to heal you. Does it? A thousand times no! The prophet Isaiah, prophesied the death of Christ decades in advance. All through the Bible the coming of the Messiah was prophesied by the prophets. The Word of God always overrides circumstances. No matter the situation all you need is a Bible verse. Why? Circumstances are subject to change, but the Word of God never changes.

CHAPTER 8

WHY SHOULD YOU PRAY?

In the beginning God created man to rule the earth. Before man had fallen from ruler ship the world was completely perfect. Heaven was made for God. The earth was made by God, for man. Man is the reason for the corruption of the world today. Many people today blame God for earthly affairs. God gave man legal rights over the earth.

THE LORD GAVE THE EARTH TO MAN

Ye are blessed of the LORD, which made heaven and earth. (Vs.16) The heaven, even the heavens, is the LORD'S: but the earth hath he given to the children of men. – **PSALM 115:15-16**

For thus saith the LORD, that created the heavens; God himself that formed the earth and made it; he hath established it, he created it not in vain, he formed it to be inhabited: I am the LORD; and there is none else.
– **ISAIAH 45:18**

And God said, Let us make man in our image, after our likeness: and **let them** have dominion over the fish of the sea, and over the fowl of the air, and over the cattle, and over all the **earth,** and over every creeping thing that creepeth upon the earth.
– **GENESIS 1:26**

When God made the statement, let them, he excluded himself. Notice, God didn't say let us. Let them means whatever happens is totally up to them. The term let them, also deals with delegated power. God wanted man to legally rule the earth. Prayer is getting God involved with what happens on earth. Why do we have to get God involved? Without a human being, God will not intervene. God will not violate his word. This is the very reason the word came into being flesh. Jesus made Christ legal on earth.

PRAYER IS AGREEMENT WITH GOD'S WILL

If my people, which are called by my name, shall humble themselves, and pray, and seek my face and turn from their wicked ways; **then** will I hear from heaven, and will forgive their sin, and will heal **their** land.
– 2 CHRONICLES 7:14

If is conditional. Notice God put specific stipulations on what is required. God said when my people do this, I will do my part. Sin is the reason the land is this way, not God. Adam and Eve didn't even know what it felt like to be ashamed before the fall. However, without prayer, God can't do anything! God is still LORD of the land, but the responsibility to rule it; he gave to man. Prayer is not begging God! Prayer is coming into agreement with God's will. What does God's will mean? The term means God's determination. God's will is his fixed purpose. God's will is what He has already decreed. God wanted things to be done in the earth as they are in heaven.

And it came to pass, that, as he (Jesus) was praying in a certain place, when he ceased, one of his disciples said unto him, Lord, teach us to pray, as John also taught his disciples. (Vs.2) And he said unto them, When ye pray, say, Our Father which art in heaven, hallowed be thy name. Thy kingdom come. Thy will be done, as in heaven, so in earth. (Vs.3) Give us day by day our daily bread. (Vs.4) And forgive us our sins; for we also forgive every one that is indebted to us. And lead us not into temptation; but deliver us from evil.
– LUKE 11:1-4

Notice, thy will be done, as in heaven; so in earth. Many translations say on earth as it is heaven. Here Jesus had not been glorified yet. Jesus wanted to keep his disciples conscience, of the Holy Spirit.

The kingdom has to come in the earth, before it can be done on the earth. The human body was created from the dust of the ground (**Genesis 2:7**). The man's body is also called an earthen vessel (**2 Corinthians 4:7**). The term earthen vessel means a clay container. God's will, have always been that the earth is like heaven. God purposed earth to be like heaven, and the end result is that it will be. Prayer is inviting God's influence on earth. Why? It is God's will. The Bible tells us to pray God's will.

f ye abide in me, and my words abide in you, ye shall ask what ye will, and it shall be done unto you. – **JOHN 15:7**

And this is the confidence that we have in him, that, if we ask any thing according to his will, he hearth us: (Vs.15) And if we know that he hear us, whatsoever we ask, we know that we have the petitions that we desired of him. - **1 JOHN 5:14-15**

(**John 15:7**): Deals with fellowship, and praying God's will. If we ask anything according to his will, he hears us. Praying God's will releases confidence. Why? God will hasten his word, and perform it (**Jeremiah 1:12**). Prayer is based on bringing God's purpose on earth. God's will is done perfectly in heaven. Everything that happens on earth is up to God's people.

THE PRAYER OF THE APOSTLES

And being let go, they went to their own company, and reported all that the chief priests and elders had said unto them. (Vs.24) And when they heard that, they lifted up their voice to God with one accord, and said, Lord, thou art God, which hast made heaven, and earth, and the sea, and all that in them is: (Vs.25) Who by the mouth of thy servant David hast said, Why did the heathen rage, and the people imagine vain things? (Vs.26) The kings of the earth stood up, and the rulers were gathered together against the Lord, and against his Christ. (Vs.27) For of a truth against thy holy child Jesus, whom thou hast anointed, both Herod, and Pontius Pilate, with the Gentiles, and the people of Israel, were gathered together, (Vs.28) For to do whatsoever thy hand and thy counsel **determined** before to be done. (Vs29) And now, Lord, behold their threatenings: and grant unto thy servants, that with all boldness they may speak thy word, (Vs.30) By stretching forth thine hand to heal; and that signs and wonders may be done by the name of thy holy child Jesus. (Vs.31) And when they had **prayed,** the place was shaken where they were assembled together; and they were all filled with the Holy Spirit, and they spake the word of God with boldness. **–ACTS 4:23-31**

The Apostles, natural reaction to a crisis was prayer. They had been commanded by the Sanhedrin council, not to speak or teach in the name of Jesus. They were threatened because of the healing that took place at the gate of the temple which is called Beautiful. Notice, after they had prayed God moved!

DAVID INQUIRED OF THE LORD

Then they told David, saying, Behold, the Philistines fight against Keilah, and they rob the threshing- floors. (Vs.2) Therefore David inquired of the LORD, saying, Shall I go and smite these Philistines? And the LORD said unto David, Go, and smite the Philistines, and save Kelilah. (Vs.3) And David's men said unto him, Behold, we be afraid here in Judah: how much more then if we come to Keilah against the armies of the Philistines? (Vs.4) Then David enquired of the LORD yet again. And the LORD answered him and said, Arise, go down to Keilah; for I will deliver the Philistines into thine hand. (Vs.5) So David and his men went to Keilah, and fought with the Philistines, and brought away their cattle, and smote them with a great slaughter. So David saved the inhabitants of Keilah. – **1 SAMUEL 23:1-5**

David was a wise man simply because he inquired of the LORD. He got the LORD involved in the affairs as pertaining to Israel. The LORD has to be granted the opportunity to get involved with the affairs of the earth. Seeking the LORD in any situation is the key to being clear of any doubt, fear, or ignorance. The Bible is crystal clear about how to obtain by faith the wisdom of God, in any situation (**James 1:5-6**). David was able to apply the wisdom of God, and save the inhabitants of Keilah.

PETER'S PRAYER RAISED THE DEAD

Now there was at Joppa a certain disciple named Tabitha, which by interpretation is called Dorcas: this woman was full of good works and almsdeeds which she did. (Vs.37) And it came to pass in those days, that she was sick, and died: whom when they had washed, they laid her in an upper chamber. (Vs.38) And forasmuch as Lydda was nigh to Joppa, and the disciples had heard that Peter was there, they sent unto him two men, desiring him that he would not delay to come to them. (Vs.39) Then Peter arose and went with them. When he was come, they brought him into the upper chamber: and all the widows stood by him weeping, and shewing the coats and garments which Dorcas made, while she was with them. (Vs.40) But Peter put them all forth, and kneeled down, and prayed, and turning him to the body said, Tabitha, arise. And she opened her eyes: and when she saw Peter, she sat up. (Vs.41) And he gave her his hand, and lifted her up, and when he had called the saints and widows, presented her alive. (Vs.42) And it was known throughout all oppa; and many believed in the Lord. (Vs.43) And it came to pass, that he arried many days in Joppa with one Simon a tanner. **– ACTS 9:36-43**

Peter put them all out, then kneeled down to pray (Vs.11). Why? Unbelief will always hinder prayer, and be a distraction in the spirit realm. Notice, that same verse **AND TURNING HIM TO THE BODY SAID TABITHA, ARISE**. Peter connected with the Holy Spirit through prayer. The Holy Spirit is the person that turned Peter's body. And the Spirit translated His words into Peter's mouth. Peter released the words of the Spirit of life, and Tabitha had to arise. Notice, Peter had to pray first, and throughout all Joppa; many believed in the Lord. The Lord's will was done.

CHAPTER 9

THE FRUIT OF THE SPIRIT

But the fruit of the Spirit is love, joy, peace, long-suffering, gentleness, goodness, faith, (Vs.23) Meekness, temperance: against such there is no law.
– **GALATIANS 5:22-23**

Agape love is what gives birth to all the other manifestations of the Spirit. There is no law against walking in Agape love. The fruit will bring about no sin. The law was given, for the knowledge of sin.

Therefore by the deeds of the law there shall no flesh be justified in his sight: for by the law is the knowledge of sin. – **ROMANS 3:20**

The Love of God, is the evidence that a person is born of God. The love of God is sacrificial.
The love of the world is consuming. The fruit of the Spirit will always manifest God.

LOVE

Beloved, let us love one another: for love is of God; and every one that loveth is born of God, and knoweth God. (Vs.8) He that loveth not knoweth not God; for God is love. (Vs.9) In this was manifested the love of God toward us, because that God sent his only begotten Son into the world, that we might live through him. (Vs.10) Herein is the love, not that we loved God, but that he loved us, and sent his Son to be the propitiation for our sins. (Vs.11) Beloved, if God so loved us, we ought also to love one another. (Vs.12) No man hath seen God at any time. If we love one another, God dwelleth in us, and his love is perfected in us. (Vs.13) Hereby know we that we dwell in him, and he in us, because he hath given us of his Spirit.
– **1 JOHN 4:7-13**

A new commandment I give unto you, That ye love one another; as I have loved you, that ye love one another. (Vs.35) By this shall all men know that ye are my disciples, if ye have love one to another.
- **JOHN 13:34-35**

By love all men shall know the Disciples of Christ. All meaning saved and the unsaved!

JOY

For our gospel came not unto you in word only, but also in power, and in the Holy Spirit, and in much assurance; as ye know what manner of men we were among you for your sake. (Vs.6) And ye became followers of us, and of the Lord, having received the word in much affliction, with joy of the Holy Spirit: (Vs.7) So that ye were ensamples.
– **1 THESSALONIANS 1:5-7**

Now the God of hope fill you with all joy, peace in believing, that ye may abound in hope through the power of the Holy Spirit. – **ROMANS 15:13**

PEACE

Peace means to join, and to set at one again. A peace of mind will come with it. However, peace of mind is not the definition.

Therefore being justified by faith, we have peace with God through our Lord Jesus Christ: (Vs.2) By whom also we have access by faith into this grace wherein we stand, and rejoice in hope of the glory of God – **ROMANS 5:1-2**

Endeavoring to keep the unity of the Spirit in the bond of peace.
– **EPHESIANS 4:3**

The manifestation of peace will keep a believer in fellowship with the LORD.

LONGSUFFERING

Put on therefore, as the elect of God, holy and beloved, bowels of mercies, kindness, humbleness of mind, meekness, longsuffering; (Vs.13) Forbearing one another, and forgiving one another, if any man have a quarrel against any: even as Christ forgave you, so also do ye.
– **COLOSSIANS 3:12-13**

The Lord is not slack concerning his promise, as some men count slackness; but long-suffering to us-ward, not willing that any should perish, but that all should come to repentance.
– **2 PETER 3:9**

Long-suffering is the given ability by the Spirit to have long patience. Long-suffering is the power of forbearance. Long-suffering is the ability not to be overthrown by afflictions!
Long-suffering is the manifestation of God. When the enemy comes he comes to get a believer out of the Spirit. Why? There is no power in the flesh.

GENTLENESS

God is my strength and power: and he maketh my way perfect. (Vs.34) He maketh my feet like hinds' feet: and setteth me upon my high places. (Vs.35) He teacheth my hands to war; so that a bow of steel is broken by mine arms. (Vs.36) Thou hast also given me the shield of thy salvation: and thy gentleness hath made me great. – **2 SAMUEL 22:33-36**

Now I Paul myself beseech you by the meekness and gentleness of Christ, who in presence am base among you, but being absent am bold toward you: (Vs.2) But I beseech you, that I may not be bold when I am present with that confidence, wherewith I think to be bold against some, which think of us as if we walked according to the flesh.
– **2 CORINTHIANS 10:1-2**

GOODNESS

Wherefore also we pray always for you, that our God would count you worthy of this calling, and fulfill all the good pleasure of his goodness, and the work of faith with power: (Vs.12) That the name of our Lord Jesus Christ may be glorified in you, and ye in him, according to the grace of our God and the Lord Jesus Christ.
– 2 THESSALONIANS 1:11-12

And I myself also am persuaded of you, my brethren, that ye also are full of goodness, filled with all knowledge, able also to admonish one another.
– ROMANS 15:14

FAITH

Holding the mystery of faith in a pure conscience.
– 1 TIMOTHY 3:9

By faith Jacob, when he was a dying, blessed both the sons of Joseph: and worshipped, leaning upon the top of his staff. **– HEBREWS 11:21**

Faith will make a believer faithful. Faith is faithfulness.

MEEKNESS

Brethren, if a man be overtaken in a fault, ye which are spiritual, restore such a one in the spirit of meekness; considering thyself, lest thou also be tempted.
– GALATIANS 6:1

Who is a wise man and endued with knowledge amongst you? Let him shew out of a good conversation his works with meekness of wisdom.
– JAMES 3:13

Meekness means humility. A believer must be humble to receive God's grace. Humbleness is the opposite of pride. Jesus Christ humbled himself, and became obedient to death. Humility is Holy Spirit power!

TEMPERANCE

Temperance deals with self-control. It is impossible to have self-control without having self-restraints. The Holy Spirit will restrict the ruling of the flesh.

Grace and peace be multiplied unto you through the knowledge of God, and of Jesus our Lord, (Vs.3) According as his divine power hath given unto us all things that pertain unto life and godliness, through the knowledge of him that hath called us to glory and virtue: (Vs.4) Whereby are given unto us exceeding great and precious promises: that by these ye might be partakers of the divine nature, having escaped the corruption that is in the world through lust. (Vs.5) And beside this, giving all diligence, add to your faith virtue; and to virtue knowledge; (Vs.6) And to knowledge temperance; and to temperance patience; and to patience godliness; (Vs.7) And to godliness brotherly kindness; and to brotherly kindness charity.
– **2 PETER 1:2-7**

CHAPTER 10

UNDERSTANDING KINGDOM AUTHORITY

A MAN UNDER AUTHORITY

And when Jesus was entered into Capernaum, there came unto him a centurion, beseeching him, (Vs.6) And saying, Lord, my servant lieth at home sick of the palsy, grievously tormented. (Vs.7) And Jesus saith unto him, I will come and heal him. (Vs.8) The centurion answered and said, Lord, I am not worthy that thou shouldest come under my roof: but speak the word only, and my servant shall be healed. (Vs.9) For I am a man under authority, having soldiers under me: and I say to this man, Go, and he goeth; and to another, Come, and he cometh; and to my servant, Do this, and he doeth it. (Vs.10) When Jesus heard it, he marveled, and said to them that followed, Verily I say unto you, I have not found so great faith, no, not in Israel. (Vs.13) And Jesus said unto the centurion, Go thy way; and as thou hast believed, so be it done unto thee. And his servant was healed in the selfsame hour.
– **MATTHEW 8:5-10, 13**

The centurion understood how kingdoms operated. The centurion was not a worshipper of the God of Israel. However, the commander understood authority. He said I am a man under authority. The centurion had the power to make people go and come at a single command. His authority was delegated from the governor Caesar! When the centurion gave a command instead of people seeing him they saw Caesar. The centurion had delegated authority. Palestine Judea that whole area was a colony. Caesar placed tetrarchs inside of the province to control the Jews. Herod and Pilate were both tetrarchs that ruled different divisions. Although the centurion wasn't a governor, he was a commander over a hundred soldiers. He was assigned to Capernaum, to keep the Jews in order. The centurion had heard, and observed the kingdom influence of Jesus Christ. And when Jesus was entered into Capernaum, there came unto him a centurion, beseeching him (Vs.5). And saying, Lord, my servant lieth at home sick of palsy, grievously tormented (Vs.6). The centurion came begging convinced that Jesus was able to heal his servant. Why? In a kingdom you speak and the Government brings it to pass. God is the Government Jesus was under.

The centurion noticed, Jesus was operating from another realm. The commander had power, but not over palsy. The centurion knew that Jesus had authority over even palsy.

JOSEPH EXALTED FOR DEFINING DREAM

And the thing was good in the eyes of Pharaoh, and in the eyes of all his servants. (Vs.38) And Pharaoh said unto his servants, Can we find such a one as this is, a man in whom the Spirit of God is? (Vs.39) And Pharaoh said unto Joseph, Forasmuch as God hath shewed thee all this, there is none so discreet and wise as thou art: (Vs.40) Thou shalt be over my house, and according unto thy word shall all my people be ruled: only in the throne will I be greater than thou. (Vs.41) And Pharaoh said unto Joseph, See, I have set thee over all the land of Egypt. (Vs.42) And Pharaoh took off his ring from his hand, and put it upon Joseph's hand, and arrayed him in vestures of fine linen, and put a gold chain about his neck; (Vs.43) And he made him to ride in the second chariot which he had; and they cried before him, Bow the knee: and he made him ruler over all the land of Egypt. (Vs.44) And Pharaoh said unto Joseph, I am Pharaoh, and without thee shall no man lift up his hand or foot in all the land of Egypt. (Vs.45) And Pharaoh called Joseph's name Zaphnathpaaneah; and he gave him to wife Asenath the daughter of Poti-pherah priest of On. And Joseph went out over all the land of Egypt.
– **GENESIS 41:37-45**

Pharaoh was the king of Egypt. A king is a ruler. A king impacts a domain with his will culture and intentions. A king has land, and subjects. A king is a sovereign. A king has laws. A king doesn't need a consultant. A king can delegate authority to whomever he desires to. Joseph was a Hebrew slave gifted by God to interpret dreams. Joseph was introduced to Pharaoh for being acknowledged as a man that could interpret dreams. Joseph was introduced to Pharaoh by the chief butler, the chief butler knew from experience that Joseph could interpret dreams (**Genesis 40:8-13**).

Pharaoh delegated power to Joseph. Pharaoh gave Joseph his ring! The ring was a signet, it contained all King Pharaoh's worth. A signet ring represents legal authority. Joseph was exalted to be prime minister over all the land of Egypt. In one instance, Joseph went from being a slave to a prime minister. Why? Cause in a kingdom a king promotes whomever he wishes. Pharaoh promoted Joseph physically. God promoted Joseph Spiritually.

It was God, that gave Pharaoh the dreams.

For the kingdom is the LORD'S: and he is the governor among the nations. – **PSALM 22:28**

THE DECREE AGAINST DANIEL

It pleased Darius to set over the kingdom an hundred and twenty princes, which should be over the whole kingdom; (Vs.2) And over these three presidents; of whom Daniel was first: that the princes might give accounts unto them, and the king should have no damage. (Vs.3) Then this Daniel was preferred above the presidents and princes, because an excellent spirit was in him; and the king thought to set him over the whole realm. (Vs.4) Then the presidents and the princes sought to find occasion against Daniel concerning the kingdom; but they could find none occasion nor fault; forasmuch as he was faithful, neither was there any error or fault found in him. (Vs.5) Then said these men, We shall not find any occasion against this Daniel, except we find it against him concerning the law of his God. (Vs.6) Then these presidents and princes assembled together to the king, and said thus unto him, King Darius, live for ever. (Vs.7) All the presidents of the kingdom, the governors, and princes, the counsellers, and the captains, have consulted together to establish a royal statute, and to make a firm decree, that whosoever shall ask a petition of any God or man for thirty days, save of thee, O king, he shall be cast into the den of lions. – **DANIEL 6:1-7**

King Darius signed the decree through ignorance. King Darius was a Median. The law of the Medes and Persians was that no decree or statute could alter. Daniel, dominated the kingdom by an excellent mind. The word excellent means preeminent. Daniel had a superior mind. The functionaries couldn't find any fault in Daniel. The officials observed that Daniel was a prayer warrior.

Now when Daniel knew that the writing was signed, he went into his house; and his windows being open in his chamber toward Jerusalem, he kneeled upon his knees three times a day, and prayed, and gave thanks before his God, as he did aforetime. (Vs.11) Then these men assembled, and found Daniel praying and making supplication before his God. (Vs.12) Then they came near, and spake before the king concerning the king's decree; Hast thou not signed a decree, that every man that shall ask a petition of any God or man within thirty days, save of thee, O king, shall be cast into the den of lions?

The king answered and said, The thing is true, according to the law of the Medes and Persians, which altereth not. (Vs.13) Then answered they and said before the king, That Daniel, which is of the Children of the captivity of Judah, regardeth not thee, O king, nor the decree that thou hast signed, but maketh his petition three times a day.
– DANIEL 6:10-13

Daniel had been ruling the Babylonian kingdom through prayer. Daniel was in right alignment with God. The tribe of Judah had been brought into captivity for failing to obey God. Daniel knew the promise of the Most High. Notice, Daniel's natural response after he knew the decree was signed was prayer. Daniel prayed and gave thanks. Notice, even in captivity, Daniel maintained giving thanks. Giving thanks was based on trusting God's integrity. Why did Daniel pray toward Jerusalem?

If they (Jews) return to thee with all their heart and with all their soul in the land of their captivity, whither they have carried them captives, and pray toward their land, which thou gavest unto their fathers, and toward the city which thou hast chosen, and toward the house which I have built for thy name: (Vs.39) Then hear thou from the heavens, even from thy dwelling place, their prayer and their supplications, and maintain their cause, and forgive thy people which have sinned against thee.
– 2 CHRONICLES 6:38-39

Daniel knew the promises. Daniel prayed and gave thanks. Daniel operated from a completely different Kingdom! King Darius was bound to a decree that couldn't be changed. Daniel also had a decree that couldn't be changed.

Then the king commanded, and they brought Daniel, and cast him into the den of lions. Now the king spake and said unto Daniel, Thy God whom thou servest continually, he will deliver thee. (Vs.17) And a stone was brought, and laid upon the mouth of the den; and the king sealed it with his own signet of his lords; that the purpose might not be changed concerning Daniel. (Vs.18) Then the king went to his place, and passed the night fasting: neither were instruments of musick brought before him: and his sleep went from him. (Vs.19) Then the king arose very early in the morning, and went in haste unto the den of lions. (Vs.20) And when he came to the den, he cried with a lamentable voice unto Daniel: and the king spake and said to Daniel, O Daniel, servant of the living God, is thy God, whom thou servest continually, able to

deliver thee from the lions? (Vs.21) Then said Daniel unto the king, O king, live for ever. (Vs.22) My God hath sent his angel, and hath shut the lions' mouths, that they have not hurt me: forasmuch as before him innocency was found in me; and also before thee, O king, have I done no hurt. (Vs.23) Then was the king exceeding glad for him, and commanded that they should take Daniel up out of the den. So Daniel was taken up out of the den, and no manner of hurt was found upon him, because he believed in his God.
– **DANIEL 6:16-23**

Daniel ended up making pillows out the lions. Daniel was found innocent in the eyes of the LORD. Daniel hadn't done any injustice to anyone. God is a God of righteousness. Whenever Israel was in right standing with God they prevailed. Whenever Israel was in defiance, the LORD God removed his hand. Daniel understood that God was just!

And the king commanded, and they brought those men which had accused Daniel, and they cast them into the den of lions, them, their children, and their wives; and the lions had the mastery of them, and brake all their bones in pieces or ever they came at the bottom of the den. (Vs.25) Then king Darius wrote unto all people, nations, and languages, that dwell in all the earth; Peace be multiplied unto you. (Vs.26) I make a decree, That in every dominion of my kingdom men tremble and fear before the God of Daniel: for he is the living God, and steadfast for ever, and his kingdom that which shall not be destroyed, and his dominion shall be even unto the end. (Vs.27) He delivereth and rescueth, and he worketh signs and wonders in heaven and in earth, who hath delivered Daniel from the power of the lions. (Vs.28) So this Daniel prospered in the reign of Darius, and in the reign of Cyrus the Persian.
– **DANIEL 6:24-28**

King Darius wrote a decree to every dominion of his kingdom which was 120 provinces. This was to keep the lions' den experience from ever happening again or any other thing as such. It was also done to make men tremble and fear before the God of Daniel. After Belshazzar the king of the Chaldeans was slain Darius the median took the kingdom.

In the first year of the reign of Darius the king, an angelic being from the LORD protected him.

Also I (Angel) in the first year of Darius the Mede, even I, stood to confirm and to strengthen him. – **DANIEL 11:1**

King Darius was encouraged, and protected to bring about the favor. King Darius was also encouraged to bring about the release of Judah from captivity. According to the promise of God, Judah was to be released from captivity after seventy years (**Jeremiah 29:10-11**). The LORD God, is able to make all things work in fulfilling His promises. The LORD God, is faithful to his kingdom and it reigns supreme. Daniel the prophet was able to have things revealed to him that allowed him to see in the future (**Daniel 9:2**).

THE UNSEEN REALM

Finally, my brethren, be strong in the Lord, and in the power of his might. (Vs.11) Put on the whole armour of God, that ye may be able to stand against the wiles of the devil. (Vs.12) For we wrestle not against flesh and blood, but against principalities, against powers, against the rulers of the darkness of this world, against spiritual wickedness in high places. **–EPHESIANS 6:10-12**

Believers must be strong in the dominion of the Lord, which comes through his word. Satan has a hierarchy that is orderly ranked to stop Christians, from exalting the name of Jesus. Specifically the principalities are the highest ranking satanic forces. The Greek word for principalities is chief. These are the ones assigned to regions to rule over and carry out Satan's plans of darkness. These are the ones that withstood the Arch angel Gabriel for twenty one days (**Daniel 10:13**). The unseen realm is just as real as the natural world. In fact the spiritual world determines what happens in the natural world. For we wrestle not against flesh and blood. Your boss is not your enemy. Your ex-spouse is not your enemy. Your Co-worker is not even your enemy. These are just puppets that the enemy does use. Through Jesus Christ, believers have been given authority over the whole hierarchy of Satan.

Behold, I give you power to tread on serpents and scorpions, and over all the power of the enemy: and nothing shall by any means hurt you. **– LUKE 10:19**

CHAPTER 11

MADE RIGHTEOUS

For he (God) hath made him (Jesus) to be sin for us, who knew no sin; that we might be made the righteousness of God in him.
– **2 CORINTHIANS 5:21**

For as by one man's disobedience many were made sinners, so by the obedience of one shall many be made righteous. – **ROMANS 5:19**

The gift of righteousness came through Jesus Christ being made sin. Jesus Christ was the propitiation for the sins of the world. Many times we often hear how God is love. God is love very true statement. God however is also just. By making Jesus to be the propitiation God was declaring his righteousness. Jesus was the word made flesh. He was Holy and innocent. Jesus laid his sinless life down as a ransom for many. What is a ransom? A ransom is a price commanded to let the captives go free. Jesus became obedient even unto death. Jesus, left heaven being one with God. Jesus became a man to take sin out of the world. Sin entered the world by a man.

For the wages of sin is death; but the gift of God is eternal life through Jesus Christ.
– **ROMANS 6:23**

Notice, the wages of sin is death. The sin is the initial sin that Adam committed. The sin of Adam brought forth the sin nature. The gift of God is eternal life through Jesus Christ. The gift of righteousness is eternal life. Eternal life is a type of life.

We know that we passed from death unto life, because we love the brethren. He that loveth not his brother abideth in death. (Vs.15) Whosoever hateth his brother is a murderer: and ye know that no murderer hath eternal life abiding in him.
– **1 JOHN 3:14-15**

Jesus answered and said unto her, Whosoever drinketh of this water shall thirst again: (Vs.14) But whosoever drinketh of the water that I shall give him shall never thirst; but the water that I shall give him shall be in him a well of water springing up into everlasting life. – **JOHN 4:13-14**

He that hates his brother is a murderer. No murderer has eternal life dwelling in him. Whosoever drinks of this water will thirst again. What did Jesus mean by that? Her water represented an ungodly life. His water represented the Holy Spirit. No matter how much drugs a sinner does, they will always desire more. The same thing is true with whatever ungodly activities they do. We were created to be fulfilled by God. Not fulfilled by God automatically gives the "Sin Nature" dominion. Why? The lust of the flesh is never satisfied. However, eternal life is the very life, and nature of God. Every human is going to live forever. Eternal life is living in the presence of God. The life that awakes a Christian will be living in God's presence as it is now. Spiritual death is separation from God. People today are alive, but they're dead at the same time.

Now she that is a widow indeed, and desolate, trusteth in God, and continueth in supplications and prayers night and day. (Vs.6) But she that liveth in pleasure is dead while she liveth.
– **1 TIMOTHY 5:5-6**

Jesus came to take away the power of the sin nature. The sin nature came through the offense of Adam. A sinner is enslaved by the sin nature. What makes a sinner a sinner? Not being born again! A person that's not born again is not a sinner because they do sinful things. The essence of a sinner is to express sinful actions. A Christian has been made righteous. A believer's true essence is to express innocence.

RESULTS OF BEING MADE RIGHTEOUS

For sin shall not have dominion over you: for ye are not under the law, but under grace. (Vs.15) What then? Shall we sin, because we are not under the law, but under grace? God forbid. Know ye not, that to whom ye yield yourselves servants to obey, his servants ye are to whom ye obey; whether of sin unto death, or of obedience unto righteousness? (Vs.17) But God be thanked, that ye were the servants of sin, but ye have obeyed from the heart that form of doctrine which was delivered you. (Vs.18) Being then made free from sin, ye became the servants of righteousness.
– **ROMANS 6:14:18**

Free from the dominion of sin is the result of being made righteous. Israel couldn't keep the law. Sacrifices were the Israelites only way to stay in somewhat right standing with God. Grace is an empowerment to rule over sin. Grace is a divine influence upon the heart. Grace shouldn't make a person want to sin. Grace is designed to make a person not want to sin. A converted believer is a servant of righteousness. The word righteousness means justification. That's where we get the word just from. The word also means innocent. A believer is acquitted of the offense that Adam brought about.

Whosoever abideth in him sinneth not: whosoever sinneth hath not seen him, neither know him. (Vs.7) Little children, let no man deceive you: he that doeth righteousness is righteous, even as he is righteous. (Vs.8) He that committeth sin is of the devil; for the devil sinneth from the beginning. For this purpose the Son of God was manifested, that he might destroy the works of the devil. (Vs.9) Whosoever is born of God doth not commit sin; for his seed remaineth in him: and he cannot sin, because he is born of God. (Vs.10) In this the children of God are manifest, and the children of the devil: whosoever doeth not righteousness is not of God, neither he that loveth not his brother.
– 1 JOHN 3:6-10

Jesus came to destroy the works of the devil. The works of the devil are the dead seed. A believer cannot sin, because God's seed is in him. This means he can't **live in sin**. Whoever does righteousness is righteous, as he is righteous. The believer is made the righteousness of God in Christ Jesus. Justification by faith means a believer is made to be righteous.
Righteousness means equitable in character or act. Many believers really don't understand being made righteous. Majority defines it as I'm saved now, and I can live however I want. Or I said the prayer the hard part is over. A false doctrine will always create a false lifestyle!

Therefore if any man be in Christ, he is a new creature: old things are passed away; behold, all things are become new. – **2 CORINTHIANS 5:17**

Behold is the key word in this verse. Behold means lo, see. It's an expression that calls attention to an amazing event. Behold means there is evidence that's following a born again person. Old things have passed away. The dead seed has passed away. Condemnation has passed away. Hatred has passed away.
If is conditional. If any man is in Christ, he is a new creation.

Created as righteousness! A manufacturer creates a product to perform at his desired standard.

THE DANGER OF SELF RIGHTEOUSNESS

Brethren, my heart's desire and prayer to God for Israel is, that they might be saved. (Vs.2) For I bear them record that they have a zeal of God, but not according to knowledge. (Vs.3) For they being ignorant of God's righteousness, and going about to establish their own righteousness, have not submitted themselves unto the righteousness of God. (Vs.4) For Christ is the end of the law for righteousness to every one that believeth.
– **ROMANS 10:1-4**

The law fulfilled its purpose by bringing us to Christ. Christ is the end of the law for righteousness. Those who believe have fulfilled righteousness through him. It's dangerous for a person not to have knowledge of God's righteousness. Why? They will always create a righteousness of their own.

The Israelites were prime examples! Self-righteousness is always based on a system that God doesn't approve of. The Israelites were so hung up on the customs that came with the law. The customs allowed them to miss the person it was all about. You know, the same thing is true in modern day Christianity.

Many professing believers have never submitted themselves to God's righteousness. Whenever this happens religion is inevitable. For a person to sing loudly, in a service with un-forgiveness in their heart is self-righteousness. A judgmental person is self- righteous! Living like a Christian one day out of the week is self-righteousness.

The list goes on. These things are a result of not being made righteous. Righteousness is imputed. The righteousness received is life changing.

SELF RIGHTEOUSNESS CARETH NOT

And, behold, there was a woman which had a spirit of infirmity eighteen years, and was bowed together, and could in no wise lift up herself. (Vs.12) And when Jesus saw her, he called her to him, and said unto her, Woman, thou art loosed from thine infirmity. (Vs.13) And he laid his hands on her: and immediately she was made straight, and glorified God. (Vs.14) And the ruler of the synagogue answered with indignation, because that Jesus had healed on the Sabbath day, and said unto the people, There are six days in which men ought to work: in them therefore come and be healed, and not on the Sabbath day. (Vs.15) The Lord then answered him, and said, Thou hypocrite, doth not each one of you on the Sabbath loose his ox or his ass from the stall, and lead him away to watering? And ought not this woman, being a daughter of Abraham, whom Satan hath bound, lo, these eighteen years, be loosed from this bond on the Sabbath day? And when he had said these things, all his adversaries were ashamed: and all the people rejoiced for all the glorious things that were done by him. – **LUKE 13:11-17**

The self-righteous are heartless. Those that live externally have nothing going internally. The Pharisees, and Scribes were living with a system that the LORD God, did not approve of. They often tried to look for wrongdoings of the Lord Jesus. This is a common thing in modern day religion. The Pharisees, and Scribes were condemned. Guilty of the sin of Adam, they were not born again. Condemned people try to condemn people! Whenever folks are not lined up with God's word they seek to condemn others. The ruler of the synagogue, cared less that this woman was bound by Satan for eighteen years. His only concern was why is healing taken place on the Sabbath day. Not a sign of the fruit of the Spirit whatsoever. Many times people think serving God is about keeping a bunch of rules. That is not even in a good range of the truth. It's all about Christ living his life through his purchased vessel. The law was written on tablets of stone. The law was external. The Holy Spirit writes his laws on our hearts.

Wherefore the Holy Spirit also is a witness to us: for after that he had said before, (Vs.16) This is the covenant that I will make with them after those days, saith the Lord, I will put my laws into their hearts, and in their minds will I write them; (Vs.17) And their sins and iniquities will I remember no more.
– HEBREWS 10:15-17

In context, these verses are referring to the children of Israel. Which is referring to word the LORD God, spoke through the prophet (**Jeremiah 31:33-34**). Though Israel was in covenant with the LORD God, they were not regenerated. Many times people are trying to please the LORD in the merit of the flesh. Self - efforts will always bring about bondage. The Holy Spirit writes his laws on an individual's heart, and causes them to be empowered by grace.

God only has one means for righteousness the Lord Jesus Christ. Jesus is the end of the law for righteousness (**Romans 10:4**).

The Jews, fell in love with the customs of the law, and tried to use it as a means of justification. The LORD gave the law for the knowledge of sin (**Romans 3:20**). So what is it the Holy Spirit writes upon the heart? That's right the love of God. Now where many people go wrong is that they try to isolate the love of God from the fruit of the Spirit.

But the fruit of the Spirit is love, joy, peace, longsuffering, gentleness, goodness, faith, (Vs.23) Meekness, temperance against such there is no law.
– GALATIANS 5:22-23

Now let's notice, one thing here in particular. It says the fruit of the Spirit singular, not plural. Why is that? The love of God is the egg that everything else is birthed from. Jesus said by love will all men know that you are my disciples, if you love one another (**John 13:34**).

It can be read like this, by the fruit of the Spirit, will all men know you are my disciples. Whenever we are walking in the fruit of the Spirit, we give people God encounters. It's very obvious to see when the fruit of the Spirit is not in manifestation. For instance, you can go to a Sunday service, and the person on your right side never greets you. The fruit in manifestation wouldn't allow that to happen. The fruit would have greeting taking place. One of the works of the flesh is emulations. You share what Christ has done through you. And then the person you shared it with tries to excel your mentions. This is a sign that the flesh is in operation.

CHAPTER 12

REVEALED

THE LORD HAS TO REVEAL HIMSELF

And the LORD appeared again in Shiloh: for the LORD revealed himself to Samuel in Shiloh by the word of the LORD. **– 1 SAMUEL 3:21**

The LORD appeared twice in Shiloh, to Samuel. The first appearance the Lord made was by a vision. The second time the LORD appeared by his word. The word and the LORD are one. The LORD is a mystery altogether. Samuel had a call on his life, but the LORD still had to reveal it. Reveal means to take the cover off. Reveal also means to disclose.

It's impossible for anyone to know the LORD unless he reveals himself. Sinners don't have the foggiest idea about the LORD. The LORD reveals himself through his word! The word of God is equal to a visual encounter. The word of God contains vision. The word of the LORD allows a person to see what the LORD sees.

KEEPING WHAT HAS BEEN REVEALED

For I am not ashamed of the gospel of Christ: for it is the power of God unto salvation to every one that believeth; to the Jew first, and also to the Greek. (Vs.17) For therein is the righteousness of God revealed from faith to faith: as it is written, The just shall live by faith. **– ROMANS 1:16-17**

The gospel was revealed to the Jews first. The gospel was first preached to Abraham. God told Abraham in him shall all nations be blessed. Then the gospel came to the non-Jewish people. God has taken off the cover for all believers alike. Those that are justified are supposed to live by what has been exposed to them. A believer has been given knowledge to know the mysteries of God. Knowledge is always given by God to know the mysteries.

And the disciples came, and said unto him, Why speakest thou unto them in parables? (Vs.11) He answered and said unto them, Because it is given unto you to know the mysteries of the kingdom of heaven, but to them it is not given. – **MATTHEW 13:10-11**

Let a man so account of us, (Apostles) as of the ministers of Christ, and stewards of the mysteries. **– 1 CORINTHIANS 4:1**

The mysteries of the kingdom, have to be revealed by God, through the Lord Jesus Christ. All believers have been granted revelation, and are responsible for managing it. This is why the Lord Jesus commissioned all his apostles to go into all of the world, and preach the gospel to every creature (**Mark 15:16**).

THE CHURCH WAS FOUNDED UPON REVELATION

When Jesus came into the coasts of Caesarea Philippi, he asked his disciples, saying, Whom do men say that I the Son of man am? (Vs.14) And they said, Some say that thou art John the Baptist: some, Elias; and others, Jeremias, or one of the prophets. (Vs.15) He saith unto them, But whom say ye that I am? (Vs.16) And Simon Peter answered and said, Thou art the Christ, the Son of the living God. (Vs.17) And Jesus answered and said unto him, Blessed art thou, Simon Barjona: for flesh and blood hath not revealed it unto thee, but my Father which is in heaven. (Vs.18) And I say also unto thee, That thou art Peter, and upon this rock I will build my church: and the gates of hell shall not prevail against it. (Vs.19) And I will give unto thee the keys of the kingdom of heaven: and whatsoever thou shalt bind on earth shall be bound in heaven: and whatsoever thou shalt loose on earth shall be loosed in heaven.
– MATTHEW 16:13-19

Notice, how all the other people guessed who Jesus was. They guessed from sense knowledge. Revelation was given to Peter's spirit directly from God. Revelation is the ability to know something that you didn't have a clue about a minute earlier. Jesus said upon this rock I will build my church. The word church means called out ones. Upon the revelation of knowing who Jesus is the gates of hell will not prevail against it. People are saved by knowing who Jesus Christ is. And they are not locked in the gates of the dead.

The word hell in the Greek means hades, the place of departed souls. Spiritual death or the abode of the wicked does not prevail against the church. The keys of the kingdom can lock things up, and they can unlock things! The keys are accessed to another realm. The kingdom is God, and revelation is God.

The church is founded upon revelation. Believers have the ability to understand God's word. You ever seen an unsaved person try to read God's word? They can't understand it. Why? God hasn't revealed himself to them. By the gospel, God is revealed from faith to faith. Because the church was established upon revelation, it has to be sustained by revelation. God has submitted himself to giving the church revelation. Every time you read God's word and you get a revelation God has revealed it. The revelation has always been there. But God has revealed it so you can get it. Visions are God manifesting himself. Visions reveal what's already done. A believer is wired from Spiritual birth to want to see God manifest himself. It's in our spiritual DNA.

WITHOUT THE WORD THERE IS NO REVELATION

Where there is no vision, the people perish: but he that keepeth the law, happy is he.
– PROVERBS 29:18

The word brings about vision. The scripture could read like this, and it wouldn't do it any injustice. Where there is no revelation the people perish: but he that keeps the law, happy is he. The Hebrew word for vision means revelation! Where the people have no redemptive revelation of God, they perish (**Amos 8:11-13**).

My people are destroyed for lack of knowledge: because thou hast rejected knowledge, I will also reject thee, that thou shalt be no priest to me: seeing thou hast forgotten the law of thy God, I will also forget thy children.
– HOSEA 4:6

My people are destroyed for a lack of discernment. Whenever God's word is rejected, God is rejected. Whenever God's word is rejected, people lose their positions. The word priest means officiate! The Jews were commanded to teach their children about God. So when they rejected God, he rejected them, and their children. Why? God is one with his word. A carnal mind opposes the word of God. So their children were denied access to God's word. That is because the parents were denying God!

THE LIGHT OF THE LORD

In him was life; and the life was the light of men. **– JOHN 1:4**

For with thee is the fountain of life: in thy light shall we see light.
– PSALM 36:9

Believers have been quickened by the word of God. The word of God is the light of God. The word is a constant supply of life in the Spirit. In the Spirit there is light. Light produces after its own kind. To them that have, much more light will be given! Light is nothing more than revelation. The revelation that's kept is the revelation that increases. Believers have been illuminated by the word.
For ye were sometimes in darkness, but now are ye light in the in the Lord: walk as children of light: (Vs.9) For the fruit of the Spirit is in all goodness and righteousness and truth; Proving what is acceptable unto the Lord. (Vs.11) And have no fellowship with the unfruitful works of darkness, but rather reprove them. **– EPHESIANS 5:8-11**

Every good gift and every perfect gift is from above, and cometh down from the Father of lights, with whom is no variableness, neither shadow of turning. (Vs.18) Of his own will begat he us with the word of truth, that we should be a kind of firstfruits of his creatures. **– JAMES 1:17-18**

The Father of lights, has recreated the spirit of all his children, by the word of truth. What is the word of truth? The word of truth is the glorious gospel of Christ, the righteousness of God. The Father God, has placed his children of light in the middle of a dark world to radiate his presence. As samples to what he has consecrated through Christ Jesus to himself. The LORD wants his children to reprove those that are in darkness. You ever notice, how sinners watch a believer's every step? And why do they do this? A sinner is separated from God, from the cause of a dead seed. However, sinners watch Christians to see how they really live.

A sinner is condemned because of the transgression of Adam. They naturally will flee, and be in complete opposition to the things of God. So they watch a believer carefully, and when they see that they're not living the life of a born again person what happens? They reject all access of the quote unquote Christian to minister to them. However, a sinner will come to a believer that they see Christ living through and ask for prayer in time of emergency. Why? A person period will always rely on someone they can trust. And people will always make an escape from those they don't trust.

CHAPTER 13

THE SUBMITTED TONGUE

NO HUMAN POWER CAN TAME THE TONGUE

For every kind of beasts, and of birds, and of serpents, and of things in the sea, is tamed, and hath been tamed of mankind: (Vs.8) But the tongue can no man tame; it is an unruly evil, full of deadly poison. (Vs.9) Therewith bless we God, even the Father; and therewith curse we men, which are made after the similitude of God. (Vs.10) Out of the same mouth proceedeth blessing and cursing. My brethren, these things ought not so to be. (Vs.11) Doth a fountain send forth at the same place sweet water and bitter? **– JAMES 3:7-11**

The tongue cannot be tamed by any man. This means by human virtue. The tongue is an unruly member. The tongue is difficult to control or subdue. It will not be managed by human strength. This is why gossiping takes course, so easily. Gossip is everywhere, even in the house of God. Yes, that's right, after the prayer service. Why is that? The tongue can only be controlled by the power of the Holy Spirit. The tongue enslaves people that have no control. Meditating on the word will give a believer power over the tongue. Meditate means to mutter. Muttering God's word will activate the conscience. The Spirit will make us aware of things that are contrary to his will. However, meditating takes discipline. The discipline is well while worth it. A submitted tongue will bless people. A submitted tongue will release sweet water. A submitted tongue will depart from bitter water. Bitter water symbolizes words that are contrary to God's.

THE DANGER OF WRONG WORDS

Thou art snared with the words of thy mouth, thou art taken with the words of thy mouth.
– PROVERBS 6:2

Many believers reap calamity because of the words they have sown. Do you know our words can do us more harm than the devil? Satan can't do anything to a person that speaks in line with God's word. A snare is a noose liked trap that catches birds. The word taken in that verse, means to be captured!

With your words you are captured. Does it sound like the devil needs to do anything? From the fall the tongue will naturally submit to an ungodly speech.

Whosoever keepeth his mouth and his tongue keepeth his soul from troubles.
– PROVERBS 21:23

Whosoever guards his mouth and his words keep his soul from troubles. Words and actions will always work together.

I said, I will take heed to my ways, that I sin not with my tongue: I will keep my mouth with a bridle, while the wicked is before me. **– PSALMS 39:1**

The mouth has to be guarded! And the only way it's possible is by speaking God's word. A bridle is a piece of equipment used to direct a horse.

There is that speaketh like the piercings of a sword: but the tongue of the wise is health.
– PROVERBS 12:18

Death and life are in the power of the tongue: and they that love it shall eat the fruit thereof.
– PROVERBS 18:21

GOD DOESN'T AGREE WITH WRONG WORDS

Why does God want us to speak his word? The first reason is so that we don't ruin our lives. The second reason is so we don't deceive ourselves. Remember sweet water and bitter water ought not so to be. God has commanded us to speak his word.

Let no corrupt communication proceed out of your mouth, but that which is good to the use of edifying, that it may minister grace unto the hearers.
– EPHESIANS 4:29

God wants our words to have a divine influence upon the hearts of the hearers. When our words are his words, they will edify. A sound relationship with God, starts once the tongue is submitted. It's hard for a person to walk in their faith when they don't speak faith filled words. Whatever you keep hearing you'll eventually believe. You ever want to find out what you believe? Listen to the words you're speaking. You ever want to find out what someone else believes? Listen to the words they're speaking.

If any man among you seem to be religious, and bridleth not his tongue, but deceiveth his own heart this man's religion is vain. **– JAMES 1:26**

LORD I cry unto thee: make haste unto me; give ear unto my voice, when I cry unto thee. (Vs.2) Let my prayer be set forth before thee as incense; and the lifting up of my hands as the evening sacrifice. (Vs.3) Set a watch, O LORD, before my mouth; keep the door of my lips. **– PSALM 141:1-3**

The easiest person to ever deceive is one's self. No one believes you more than you believe yourself. This is the reason a person can always talk themselves out the being healed or the blessing of God. You know, even under the Old Covenant, King David was even conscience about the perverseness of the tongue. The tongue can only be subdued by God's word. Notice, the man that doesn't do so religion is in vain (profitless).

CHAPTER 14

THE LAW OF SERVANT HOOD

THE SERVANT IS THE GREATEST

And he (Jesus) came to Capernaum: and being in the house he asked them, What was it that ye disputed among yourselves by the way? (Vs.34) But they held their peace: for by the way they had disputed among themselves, who should be the greatest. (Vs.35) And he sat down, and called the twelve, and saith unto them, If any man desire to be first, the same shall be last of all, and servant of all. – **MARK 9:33-35**

The disciple had the wrong interpretation of the greatest. In their minds they wanted to outrank each other. The disciples were steeped in Judaism. Actually, that's all they ever knew. Jesus Christ came to introduce his students to a kingdom concept. In the natural realm to outrank a person means you're greater than them. In the kingdom the servant is the greatest. In the natural when dinner is served, I eat first. In the kingdom I serve everyone first, and then I eat last. In the natural realm you hate your enemies. In the kingdom you pray for your enemies. Being a servant deals with putting others first. The kingdom concept goes against the way a person has been trained to live in. Serving others first, goes against pride. The best way to stay humble is putting other people first. Arrogance is based on a person exalting their self above others. So in the kingdom everything is reversed.

Even as the Son of man came not to be ministered unto, but to minister, and to give his life a ransom for many. – **MATTHEW 20:28**

Jesus came not to be served, but to serve. Jesus came to pay the price to let the captives go free. Being served was not a part of his agenda. The creator became a man. Jesus Christ became a human being just to serve. A humble person will always be exalted by God.

Likewise, ye younger, submit yourselves unto the elder. Yea, all of you be subject one to another, and be clothed with humility: for God resisteth the proud, and giveth grace to the humble. (Vs.6) Humble yourselves therefore under the mighty hand of God, that he may exalt you in due time: (Vs.7) Casting all your care upon him: for he careth for you. **– 1 PETER 5:5-7**

The Father, has set positions of authority in the church. The humility is being able to stay submitted to the protocol in which the Father, has structured to be relevant. God resists the proud, simply because they place themselves in complete opposition; to the counsel in which he has determined after his own will. When believers humble themselves, God exalts them in the time that they can become able to steward the positions.

JESUS WAS HUMBLE JESUS WAS EXALTED

Let this mind be in you, which was also in Christ Jesus: (Vs.6) Who, being in the form of God, thought it not robbery to be equal with God: (Vs.7) But made himself of no reputation, and took upon him the form of a servant, and was made in the likeness of men: (Vs.8) And being found in fashion as a man, he humbled himself, and became obedient unto death, even the death of the cross. (Vs.9) Wherefore God also hath highly exalted him, and given him a name which is above every name: (Vs.10) That at the name of Jesus every knee should bow, of things in heaven, and things in earth, and things under the earth; (Vs.11) And that every tongue should confess that Jesus Christ is Lord, to the glory of God the Father. **– PHILIPPIANS 2:5-11**

Christ Jesus didn't think it was robbery to be equal with God. Christ Jesus made himself of no reputation. He took on the form of a bond servant. When Christ left heaven he became a man. Jesus made Christ legal on earth! Everything Jesus did in his earthly ministry, he did all by the power of God. Every miracle Jesus did it was in total reliance on God's power. Jesus couldn't do a single miracle of his own. God exalted Jesus Christ. God gave Jesus a name that is above every name. Jesus took his blood into the Holy place, and sprinkled it on the mercy seat. The day Jesus sat down, he received the great name. The right hand of God, denotes a place of supremacy. Jesus Christ fulfilled the will of God in an orderly fashion.

The eyes of your understanding being enlightened; that ye may know what is the hope of his calling and what the riches of the glory of his inheritance in the saints, (Vs.19) And what is the exceeding greatness of is power to us-ward who believe, according to the working of his mighty power, (Vs.20) Which he wrought in Christ, when he raised him from the dead, and set him at his own right hand in the heavenly places, (Vs.21) Far above all principality, and power, and might, and dominion, and every name that is named, not only in this world, but also in that which is to come: (Vs.22) And hath put all things under his feet, and gave him to be the head over all things to the church, (Vs.23) Which is his body, the fullness of him that filleth all in all.
– EPHESIANS 1:18-23

God set him at his own right hand. Jesus was exalted. His name was exalted.

HUMILITY FIRST-THEN EXALTATION

But Jehoshaphat said, Is there not here a prophet of the LORD, that we may inquire of the LORD by him? And one of the king of Israel's servant answered and said, Here is Elisha the son of Shaphat, which poured water on the hands of Elijah. **– 2 KINGS 3:11**

Elisha was known for service first, then he got the mantle! God makes us great servants first then he exalts us. Many times we just want to have step ten, without step one. God has to build character, and faithfulness first. Why?

The worst thing that can happen, is an unfaithful person without character; be put in a place of authority. Many times believers don't want to submit to the man or woman of God, that the Father, has placed in position; so that they can partake of the leaders anointing.

CHAPTER 15

FORGIVE

WE HAVE TO FORGIVE

For if ye forgive men their trespasses, your heavenly Father will also forgive you: (Vs.15) But if ye forgive not men their trespasses, neither will your Father forgive your trespasses. **– MATTHEW 6:14-15**

Therefore I say unto you, What things soever ye desire, when ye pray, believe that ye receive them, and ye shall have them. (Vs.25) And when ye stand praying, forgive, if ye have ought against any: that your Father also which is in heaven may forgive you your trespasses. (Vs.26) But if ye do not forgive, neither will your Father which is in heaven forgive your trespasses.
–MARK 11:24-26

UN-forgiveness is the key that locks up heaven. If we don't forgive God can't forgive us. If God can't forgive a believer that means he's stuck in his sins. When a believer is stuck in his sins he's naturally dominated by the flesh. Many people have gotten divorced behind un-forgiveness! Numerous families have parted ways because of un-forgiveness! However, God looks on the heart. When we pray we are supposed to forgive. This purpose is for heart protection. Only in God's presence can forgiveness take place. Why? In God's presence you can forgive, and forget. God doesn't only forgive us he forgets. Many times people never forgive. They may say they do, but when they get mad they bring up the matter. That is not forgiveness! Jesus was informing covenant people to forgive.

Let all bitterness, and wrath, and anger, and clamour, and evil speaking, be put away from you, with all malice: (Vs.32) And be ye kind one to another, even as God for Christ's sake hath forgiven you. **– EPHESIANS 4:31-32**

Bitterness is the link that starts the chain. Bitterness will cause all the other actions to take place in that order. Bitterness means to pack or press down. In order not to forgive you have to keep reminding yourself of the offense. Or what you consider to have been an offense. Bitterness means un-forgiveness has already taken its course. Believers can forgive, just as God has forgiven us for Christ's sake. God has forgiven us on the account of Jesus. Jesus was innocent, and had never sinned. This is the reason why God can't forgive those who don't forgive. The power of being born again is the supreme power to forgive. Forgiveness is the foundation for a genuine, and an unhindered walk with the Father God, through Christ Jesus. The apostles' were put into prison, flogged cast out of cities despised, and rejected yet they walked in forgiveness.

GUARD YOUR HEART

Keep thy heart with all diligence; for out of it are the issues of life. **– PROVERBS 4:23**

UN-forgiveness comes from within. Pride is the reason professing believers don't forgive. Unbelievers have the nature of the devil. Unbelievers naturally are enslaved by un-forgiveness. Keep thy heart with all diligence. Means cautiously guard your fellowship with God. Out of the mind the issues of life are created.

And he (Jesus) said, That which cometh out of a man, that defileth the man. (Vs.21) For from within, out of the heart of men, proceed evil thoughts, adulteries, fornications, murders, (Vs.22) Thefts, covetousness, wickedness, deceit, lasciviousness, an evil eye, blasphemy, pride, foolishness: (Vs.23) All these evil things come from within, and defile the man. **– MARK 7:20-23**

In context, Jesus was addressing the Pharisees, and Scribes for asking him why his disciples didn't wash their hands before they ate; in which was held to the tradition of the elders. The Pharisees, and Scribes though they fasted, and seemed very holy outwardly they were not regenerated. Their spirit, soul, and body, was all in total agreement to carry out the will of Satan. Out the spirit (Mind) Jesus said all these things come forth and defile a man. Why? Your thoughts will always become your actions if you think about them long enough.

Eat thou not the bread of him that hath an evil eye, Neither desire thou his dainty meats: (Vs.7) For as he thinketh in his heart, so is he: Eat and drink, saith he to thee; But his heart is not with thee. (Vs.8) The morsel which thou hast eaten shalt thou vomit up, And lose thy sweet word.
– PROVERBS 23:6-8

As a man thinks in his heart so is he. The Hebrew word for heart is mind. In other words a man becomes his thoughts. This is talking about the mind, their spirits were not regenerated in the Old Testament. Don't eat the bread of him that has an evil eye. What is the meaning of the term evil eye? It means hard grudging, and envious eye.

And David went out whithersoever Saul sent him, and behaved himself wisely: and Saul set him over the men of war, and he was accepted in the sight of all the people, and also in the sight of Saul's servants. (Vs.6) And it came to pass as they came, when David was returned from the slaughter of the Philistine, that the women came out of all cities of Israel, singing and dancing, to meet king Saul, with tabrets, with joy, and with instruments of musick.(Vs.7) And the women answered one another as they played, and said, Saul hath slain his thousands, And David his ten thousands. (Vs.8) And Saul was wroth, and the saying displeased him; and he said, They have ascribed unto David ten thousands, and to me they have ascribed but thousands: and what can he have more but the kingdom? (Vs.9) And Saul eyed David from that day and forward. **– 1 SAMUEL 18:5-9**

King Saul looked at David with a jealous eye, from that day forth. He became his thoughts, and they fashioned the issues that came into his life. Thoughts come into being actioned.

CHAPTER 16

THE MEANING OF TESTIMONY

The law of the LORD is perfect, converting the soul: the testimony of the LORD is sure, making wise the simple. **– PSALM 19:7**

He that cometh from above is above all: he that is of the earth is earthly, and speaketh of the earth: he that cometh from heaven is above all. (Vs.32) And what he hath seen and heard, that he testifieth; and no man receiveth his testimony. **– JOHN 3:31-32**

The word testimony, and witness are synonymous terms. The word of the LORD is the witness of the LORD. The witness of the LORD is the testimony of the LORD. The Holy Spirit is also the witness. The Father, the Word, and the Holy Spirit, testify of the same thing. These three are one.

For there are three that bear record in heaven, the Father, the Word, and the Holy Spirit: and these three are one. **– 1 JOHN 5:7**

Many times believers come together, and tell their testimonies. We are told to make known his deeds among the people. However, testimony in the Bible means something totally different. Testimony means a believer's witness concerning the Lord Jesus Christ. A testimony is a lifestyle of being a witness. Not believers telling how they received salvation.

And they (Saints) overcame him (Satan) by the blood of the Lamb and the word of their testimony; and they loved not their lives unto the death.
– REVELATION 12:11

This is already done in the Spirit. Notice, how they prevailed against Satan? The blood of the Lamb which means they were saved by it. They also lived under the blood. Notice, the word of their testimony. Word in the verse means logos. Word there refers to Christ Jesus. Testimony in the verse means witness. One of the definitions for testimony is also a martyr. What does martyr mean? It means a person who willingly suffers death rather than renounce his or her beliefs. You can remember the Apostle Peter denied Jesus Christ. Peter denied Jesus Christ before he had been converted. After Peter's conversion, he was made into a witness!

But ye shall receive power, after that the Holy Spirit is come upon you: and ye shall be witnesses unto me both in Jerusalem, and in all Judaea, and in Samaria, and unto the uttermost part of the earth. **–ACTS 1:8**

Notice, you shall be witnesses. He didn't say you will do witnessing. There's a big difference between witnessing, and being a witness. Just like there's a difference between someone who drinks, and an alcoholic. After that the Holy Spirit has come upon you, He will make you a testimony.

Moreover if thy brother shall trespass against thee, go and tell him his fault between thee and him alone: if he shall hear thee, thou hast gained thy brother. (Vs.16) But if he will not hear thee, then take with thee one or two more, that in the mouth of two or three witnesses every word may be established.
– MATTHEW 18:15-16

Notice, that the witnesses establish truth. Their words are trustworthy. Why is that? Witnesses are just. Witnesses speak the counsel of God. A witness is an identity. A witness is one with the Holy Spirit. Glory to the Most High! A witness need to have other witnesses. This is the LORD'S will. Notice the words of the Apostle Paul in his defense before the Jews.

And it came to pass, that, when I was come again to Jerusalem, even while I prayed in the temple, I was in a trance; (Vs.18) And saw him saying unto me, Make haste, and get thee quickly out of Jerusalem: for they will not receive thy testimony concerning me. (Vs.19) And I said, Lord, they (Jews) know that I imprisoned and beat in every synagogue them that believed on thee: (Vs.20) And when the blood of thy martyr Stephen was shed, I also was standing by, and consenting unto his death, and kept the raiment of them that slew him.
– ACTS 22:17-20

Paul here mentioned previous conditions. The Lord told Paul that the Jews would not receive his testimony concerning Him. Not the testimony concerning Paul. High light what was said about Stephen. He was martyred. Why? Stephen was made a witness. It was a normal thing to be martyred for your faith in those days. Again, notice the word testimony here.

By faith Enoch was translated that he should not see death; and was not found, because God had translated him: for before his translation he had this testimony that he pleased God.
– HEBREW 11:5

Enoch was a witness. His lifestyle proved that he knew God. It doesn't say he went around telling everybody he was saved. A true witness has a lifestyle that testifies! Enoch glorified God.

Let your light so shine before men, that they may see your good works, and glorify your Father which is in heaven. **– MATTHEW 5:16**

Notice, the evidence is the light! The light shines before men. That signifies the saved, and the unsaved both will see it. God is glorified when a sinner makes mention of what they see in a sanctified believer! A witness is obvious! Remember Jesus said you will be a witness unto me. That's a legal term. In a court room they form conclusions based on evidence. Why is that? A person can say anything. But the evidence is the proof.

The LORD hath sworn in truth unto David; he will not turn from it; Of the fruit of thy body will I set upon thy throne. (Vs.12) If thy children will keep my covenant and my testimony that I shall teach them, their children shall also sit upon thy throne for evermore. **– PSALM 132:11-12**

And I, brethren, when I came to you, came not with excellency of speech or of wisdom, declaring unto you the testimony of God. **– 1 CORINTHIANS 2:1**

And it came to pass in Iconium, that they went both together into the synagogue of the Jews, and so spake, that a great multitude both of the Jews and also of the Greeks believed. (Vs.2) But the unbelieving Jews stirred up the Gentiles, and made their minds evil affected against the brethren. (Vs.3) Long

time, therefore abode they (Paul and Barnabas) speaking boldly in the Lord, which gave testimony unto the word of his grace, and granted signs and wonders to be done by their hands.
– ACTS 14:1-3

Number one, God testifies of his testimony in the Covenant he established with David. Number two, the Apostle Paul testifies of the testimony of God, to the saints at Ephesus. Number three, Apostle Paul, and Barnabas testified of the testimony of God in Iconium. God is one with his Word. The Word is a witness. The Holy Spirit is a witness. Apostle Paul was a witness. The Apostle Barnabas was a witness. The Holy Spirit came to make witnesses! The church only testifies of the testimony of God! A born again believer is made a testimony!

BEING MARTYRED FOR THE CONFESSION OF CHRIST

These things have I spoken unto you, that ye should not be offended. (Vs.2) They shall put you out of the synagogues: yea, the time cometh, that whosoever killeth you will think that he doeth God service. (Vs.3) And these things will they do unto you, because they have not known the Father, nor me. (Vs.4) But these things have I told you, that when the time shall come, ye may remember that I told you of them. And these things I said not unto you at the beginning, because I was with you. (Vs.5) But now I go my way to him that sent me; and none of you asketh me, Whither goest thou? (Vs.6) But because I have said these things unto you, sorrow hath filled your heart. (Vs.7) Nevertheless I tell you the truth; It is expedient for you that I go away: for if I go not away, the Comforter will not come unto you; but if I depart, I will send him unto you.
– JOHN 16:1-7

The Lord Jesus told his disciples that they would be put out of the synagogues, and even killed, so that they wouldn't be offended. The word offended in the Greek means to stumble or fall away. Why did he say that? Jesus told his disciples so when the time came they wouldn't fall away from their confession of him as Lord. Jesus told them that the devout Jews, would put them out of the synagogues; and even they would be killed because the Jews didn't know him or the Father. The Lord also mentioned that they would through ignorance, think they were doing God a sacred service, by doing so.

The Lord told the disciples because these Jews, lacked revelation these things were inevitable.

Now about that time Herod the king stretched forth his hands to vex certain of the church. (Vs.2) And he killed James the brother of John with the sword. (Vs.3) And because he saw it pleased the Jews, he proceeded further to take Peter also. (Then were the days of unleavened bread).
– ACTS 12:1-3

James the brother of John, sons of Zebedee an apostle who walked within the inner circle of Christ, was martyred for the sakes of the gospel. Herod the king seen that his injustice acts pleased the Jews, so he proceeded to take the life of Peter also. Peter was kept in prison, but prayer was made without ceasing of the church to God for him (**Acts 12:5**). The same night that Herod would have brought Peter forth, an angel led him out the prison. Notice, not ceasing to pray, is what got God involved on Peter's behalf.

CHAPTER 17

GO MINISTERING SPIRITS

BELIEVERS OUTRANK ANGELS

The Spirit itself (Himself) beareth witness with our spirit, that we are the children of God: (Vs.17) And if children, then heirs; heirs of God, and joint-heirs with Christ; if so be that we suffer with him, that we may be also glorified together. **– ROMANS 8:16-17**

All born again believers are children of God. We are also joint-heirs with Christ. This means believers have been given the right to possess everything that belongs to Christ Jesus. We are even partakers of his very throne (**Ephesians 2:6**). The right hand of God denotes a place of authority. Believers have been made one with God, in Christ Jesus.

This automatically outranks angels of light as well as angels of darkness. Angels were created to serve. For instance, Gabriel is a messenger angel (**Daniel 10:12**). The archangel Michael was created for warring (**Revelation 12:7**). All the angels worshipped Jesus (**Hebrews 1:6**). Angels never sit in God's presence. This shows respect to God's Supreme authority.

And Zacharias said unto the angel, Whereby shall I know this? for I am an old man, and my wife well stricken in years. (Vs.19) And the angel answering said unto him, I am Gabriel, that stand in the presence of God; and am sent to speak unto thee, and to shew thee these glad tidings.
– LUKE 1:18-19

And I (John) saw the seven angels which stood before God; and to them were given seven trumpets. (Vs.3) And another angel came and stood at the altar, having a golden censer; and there was given unto him much incense, that he should offer it with the prayers of all saints upon the golden altar which was before the throne.
– REVELATION 8:2-3

UNDER THE OLD COVENANT

Under the Old Covenant angels were assigned only by God.

For he (God) shall give his angels charge over thee, to keep thee in all thy ways. (Vs.12) They shall bear thee up in their hands, lest thou dash thy foot against a stone. **– PSALM 91:11-12**

My God hath sent his angel, and hath shut the lions' mouths, that they have not hurt me: forasmuch as before him innocency was found in me; and also before thee, O king, have I done no hurt.
– DANIEL 6:22

Jesus Christ fulfilled the Old Covenant. He established the New Covenant. The New Covenant is established upon better promises (**Hebrews 8:6**). Under the Old Covenant the Jews didn't have the ability to use the name of Jesus.

UNDER THE NEW COVENANT

But to which of the angels said he at any time, Sit on my right hand, until I make thine enemies thy footstool? (Vs.14) Are they not all ministering spirits, sent forth to minister for them who shall be heirs of salvation?
– HEBREWS 1:13-14

Heir means to obtain by inheritance. In other words, believers have possessed the throne of Jesus Christ. Believers have possessed the name of Jesus. This is why we pray in the name of Jesus. One it takes away the feeling of insignificance. And two, it is our identity. Believers are accepted in the beloved (**Ephesians 1:6**). When we give an order in Jesus name, it's just as if he did it himself.

HOW IT ALL WORKS

Bless the LORD, ye his angels, that excel in strength, that do his commandments, hearkening unto the voice of his word. **– PSALM 103:20**

The ministering spirits are created to hearken unto the word of God. The word hearkening, means to hear intelligently. Believers are supposed to voice the word of God.

For instance, this is how you would pray for a family member. Ministering spirits go forth in the name of Jesus, I give you all charge over John Doe. Keep him in all his ways, bear him up in your hands, lest at any time he should dash his foot against a stone. Satan I rebuke your operations against the ministering spirits in Jesus name Amen. Satan has to obey a believer that has been recreated in Christ Jesus. Satan knows the power of the word, and he is scared of it. This is why he comes to steal the word. The angels of God through the authority of Christ are positioned to serve the children of God. If you went to a restaurant, and the waiter came to serve you, and you never ordered anything could the waiter accommodate you?

A thousand times no! Under the Old Covenant God sent his angels to do special tasks. But under the New Covenant an angel is assigned to a believer. As Peter was released from prison by the angel of the Lord, he went to Mary's house where they were all gathered praying for him.

And as Peter knocked at the door of the gate, a damsel came to hearken, named Rhonda. (Vs.14) And when she knew Peter's voice, she opened not the gate for gladness, but ran in, and told how Peter stood before the gate. (Vs.15) And they said unto her, Thou art mad. But she constantly affirmed that it was even so. Then said they, It is his angel. **– ACTS 12:13-15**

Notice, the church thought that it was Peter's angel knocking at the door. However, the angel that released Peter from prison, was sent by the Lord because of the prayers of the church. However, when the same angel departed from Peter he remained in the area.

And upon a set day Herod, arrayed in royal apparel, sat upon his throne, and made an oration unto them. (Vs.22) And the people gave a shout, saying, It is the voice of a god, and not a man. (Vs.23) And immediately the angel of the Lord smote him, because he gave not God the glory: and he was eaten of worms, and gave up the ghost. **– ACTS 12:21-23**

CHAPTER 18

THE UNKNOWN TONGUE

THE TONGUE IS UNKNOWN TO THE BELIEVER

For he that speaketh in an unknown tongue speaketh not unto men, but unto God: for no man understandeth him; howbeit in the spirit he speaketh mysteries. (Vs.3) But he that prophesieth speaketh unto men to edification, and exhortation, and comfort.(Vs.4) He that speaketh in an known tongue edifieth himself; but he that prophesieth edifieth the church.
– 1 CORINTHIANS 14:1-4

But ye, beloved, building up yourself on your most holy faith, praying in the Holy Spirit, (Vs.21) Keep yourselves in the love of God, looking for the mercy of our Lord Jesus Christ unto eternal life. **– JUDE 1:20-21**

Speaking in an unknown tongue, is the Holy Spirit putting the utterance inside the believer. The Holy Spirit does not pray, but He imparts the utterance into the believer's spirit. The Holy Spirit imparts, mysteries into the believer's spirit. The believer then can pray God's perfect will concerning the mysteries.

What are mysteries? Mysteries are secrets. Notice building up yourselves on your most holy faith. Not in but on. Building means to build upon, and to rear up. Rear up simply means to take care, and support up to maturity. It also means to be a house builder. Most holy faith means sacred faith. Speaking in this language is a gift that has to be brought to maturity. It can be illustrated like this building a brick house. Every brick you add the taller the house gets.

Every time you pray in the unknown tongue, the more you're supposed to add. Why don't people pray in tongues? They don't believe it works. The flesh will take a person right out of doing it. Or someone was teaching it was of the devil. That's absurd! Satan will fight a believer in this area more than any other one. The average prayers are mind filled prayers. Praying in the unknown tongue is a spirit filled prayer.

For if I pray in an unknown tongue, my spirit prayeth, but my understanding is unfruitful.– **1 CORINTHIANS 14:14**

The mind is barren when you speak in the unknown tongue. This is why the flesh will oppose this practice! The flesh loves to be in control. Doesn't it? Praying in the spirit quiets the soul. God is always speaking, but the flesh can be so loud you miss him. This is why fasting is also important. It makes you sensitive to God's still small voice

For we are saved by hope: but hope that is seen is not hope: for what a man seeth, why doth he yet hope for? (Vs.25) But if we hope for that we see not, then do we with patience wait for it. (Vs.26)Likewise the Spirit also helpeth our infirmities: for we know not what we should pray for as we ought: but the Spirit itself (Himself) maketh intercession for us with groanings which cannot be uttered. (Vs.27) And he that searcheth the hearts knoweth what is the mind of the Spirit, because he maketh intercession for the saints according to the will of God. – **ROMANS 8:24-27**

Notice, the verse doesn't say we don't know how to pray. We know to pray in Jesus name (**John 16:23**). The infirmities are, we don't know how to pray as we ought. There could be something going on right now in your house that you know nothing about. Something could be taking place at your job you're not aware of. However, the Holy Spirit knows everything! The Holy Spirit makes intercession for us with groaning's that can't be uttered. Groaning means to sigh. Sigh means to emit a long, deep audible breath expressing sadness. God searches the heart, and knows what the mind of the Spirit is. The Spirit grieves with the believer. He gives the believer His groaning's concerning the condition of their heart. That's when the will of God is done.

Then said the Lord to him, (Moses) Put off thy shoes from thy feet: for the place where thou standest is holy ground. (Vs.34) I have seen, I have seen the affliction of my people which is in Egypt, and I have heard their groaning, and am come down to deliver them. And now come, I will send thee into Egypt.
– ACTS 7:33-34

When Jesus therefore saw her (Mary) weeping, and the Jews also weeping which came with her, he groaned in the spirit, and was troubled, (Vs.34) And said, Where have ye laid him (Lazarus)? They said unto him, Lord, come and see. (Vs.35) Jesus wept. (Vs.36) Then said the Jews, Behold how he loved him!

(Vs.37) And some of them said, Could not this man, which opened the eyes of the blind, have caused that even this man should not have died? (Vs.38) Jesus therefore again groaning in himself cometh to the grave. It was a cave, and a stone lay upon it. **– JOHN 11:33-38**

First, notice Stephen speaking under the unction of the Holy Spirit. He referred back to the days of Moses. He said God had seen the affliction of his people in Egypt. God heard the groaning of their hearts, and came to deliver them. As we know God did do this by the hands of Moses. God searches the heart remember that? Second notice, Jesus groaned in his spirit. And He was also troubled. Then he wept! Why is that?

The Holy Spirit sighed into his spirit. The Holy Spirit was feeling the bondage of his people. The Holy Spirit expressed His feelings through Jesus. Jesus therefore again groaning in himself comes to the cave (Vs.38). The second sigh in his spirit, he raised Lazarus from the dead! Glory to the almighty God! Whenever the Holy Spirit sighs into our spirit, it's designed to bring about the will of God. Remember the Holy Spirit helps our infirmities.

We don't know how to pray as we ought! He makes intercession for us with groans that cannot be uttered. The word intercession means to intercede in behalf of. It also means to place above! The Holy Spirit groans in our spirit. So we can pray in our prayer language. You ever went into prayer, and didn't know how to approach God? Of course you did. That's when it's time to pray in the divine language. The weakness is based upon obscurity.

If any man speak in an unknown tongue, let it be by two, or at the most by three, and that by course; and let one interpret. (Vs.28) But if there be no interpreter, let him speak to himself, and to God.
– 1 CORINTHIANS 14:27-28

PROVERBS 4:7-8

Wisdom is the principal thing; therefore get wisdom: and with all thy getting get understanding. Exalt her, and she shall promote thee: she shall bring thee to honour, when thou dost embrace her.

Email Address: risensaviour43@gmail.com
Telephone Number: 941-580-7681

******* Special Thanks To *******

JADE CURRY, CHERISH GARNER, RICKY JACKSON, CURTIS WALDEN SENIOR, CURTIS WALDEN JR, JOHNELL JACKSON, DAVE DORGELUS, YECENIA MARTINEZ, MARILYN GROVES, GARY GROVES, MARIA DEL ROSARIO, TEAL WILSON, KAREEMA BRISTOL, TRAVIS MORGAN, PATTY HOLLOWAY, WENDY HARRELL, WILLIE WALDEN, BENJAMIN ROGERS, AMBER ANDERSON, JIM HICKS, CEDRIC HOUSTON, COURTNEY DASHER, MS.VALERIE DASHER, HORACE DAVIS, DARRELL MANUEL, CHARLIE WASHINGTON, APOSTLE ALE DAVIS, MICHELLE TELLONE, KENDALL BOWMAN, DIPAN VYAS, CHARDAY DUARTE, TAMMIE WALDEN

ABOUT THE AUTHOR

Renardo McCray, born in Sarasota, Florida January 27, 1981 is an anointed teacher that believes in the great commission. An all time student of the scriptures. He understands that religion cannot satisfy spiritual hunger. He also believes greatly in the edifying of the body of Christ. He knows that without revelation, it's impossible to grow and mature in God. He is a gifted author. Blessed to share with the world. He has been downloaded with revelations from the Lord Jesus Christ. Selah

Ten Questions In Review

1. Hammedatha the Agagite was the father of whom?
2. What was Tabitha's name by interpretation?
3. The Centurion's servant was sick with what?
4. What was the name king Pharaoh gave to Joseph?
5. Which tribe of Israel was the Prophet Daniel from?
6. The daughter of the lineage of Abraham had a spirit of infirmity for how long?
7. What was the reason king Saul became envious of David?
8. What time in the prison did Paul, and Silas pray, and give praise to God?
9. How many times a day did Daniel pray, and give thanks?
10. Who was the father of Elisha the Prophet?